MANTALK

Irma Kurtz

MANTALK

·

A Book for Women Only

BTB
BEECH TREE BOOKS
WILLIAM MORROW
New York

Library of Congress Cataloging-in-Publication Data

Kurtz, Irma.
   Mantalk: a book for women only.

   (Beech tree books)
   First published in 1986 as: Malespeak.
   1. Men—Psychology.   2. Men—Attitudes.   3. Sex
role.   I. Title.
HQ1090.K87   1987   305.3'1   86-14133
ISBN 0-688-06591-0

Printed in the United States of America

   2 3 4 5 6 7 8 9 10

BOOK DESIGN BY VICTORIA HARTMAN

BTB

The word "book" is said to derive from *boka*, or beech.
The beech tree has been the patron tree of writers since ancient times and represents the flowering of literature and knowledge.

For
Ian MacDonald Munro, and Jeffrey Bernard,
Donald, Don, Douglas, both Simons, Derek,
Denis, Daniel, Harri, Hank, Mook, Clive
(Spanish fly), Clive-the-good, Michael, Mike,
Michel, Jean-Pierre, Jean-Claude, Jean-
François, Jean-Marie, Thierry, Manfred,
Gustav, Giorgio, Tony, Philip, David B.,
David J., Ephraim, Nick, Carlos, Alain,
Allen, Alan, many Johns, two Williams, Will
Wills, three Patricks, four Pauls, Dick, Jay,
Larry W., Laurie, old Rich, young Rich, rich
Rich, Jack, Jim, the unfortunate Falcon-
Barker, Ted, all the Peters, Teddy, Robert,
Bobby, Bob, Francis, Frank, Matt Carney,
Billy, Antony, Adriano, Chris, Bruce, Pepo,
Irving, Julio, James, dearest Marc,
and all the other men I've known in spite of
our sexual differences

CONTENTS

INTRODUCTION

I used to think "a man" was the singular of "amen," and the answer to a maiden's prayers. When I was very young I used to think the rat was a male mouse. In maturity I discarded the first notion as girlish wishful thinking. I'm still not altogether sure about the other.

For most of the thirty-odd years of my adult life I have been a free agent among the males, watching them with affection, sometimes with distress, even horror, occasionally with hope, always with curiosity. In the beginning, my expectations of men were high: I imagined them to be as strong and gifted and altogether magnificent as they imagine themselves to be; but in time, I learned to see through to some of the facts of matters between the sexes.

Male behavior, particularly toward females, has gradually become my area of expertise. For the past six years I have been employed as an "advice columnist" to read the endless intersexual complaints from Britain and America; and to comment on them when I can. In spite of the misery males make for females, and some have made for me, I cannot find it in the remnants of my heart to condemn the entire breed as some women do, and I continue to question rigorously all evidence that 49 percent of humanity is composed of fickle, self-serving egomaniacs.

No matter how aggressive Mantalk sounds, it is not designed for attack, but for self-defense. As a general rule, the more a man blusters, the more afraid he is of being found out to be afraid.

This work is an interpretive look at the differences between the sexes. It is my own analysis of primary source material and observations I myself have made among the men. I don't pretend to be fluent in the language men speak. Fluency depends to some extent on the experience of the listener as well as the speaker, and I can only imagine what it feels like to be a man; I am no more bilingual than I am bisexual. This is not a dictionary, but an examination of the roots and branches of Mantalk: why men say the things they do, and why women hear them say the things they are not saying, which is a phenomenon to be expected between sexes that are opposite. For example, when a woman hears a man say, "My wife doesn't understand me,'' if she has a rudimentary knowledge of Mantalk she knows that in fact he has said, "I don't understand my wife."

There has never been such a thing as objectivity, certainly not when the sexes look at each other, and so there will be people who find this report prejudiced. Some of them are going to say this is because I am unmarried, an old fruit shriveling on the vine. In Mantalk the words are: "She's a dyke. All she needs is a good screw." This, it happens, is not the case. I'm no more in need of a good screw than millions and millions of other females. I am neither a lesbian nor a disappointed spinster. Lesbianism is too sensitive, too earnest, too moist, soppy, and lacking in thrust for my temperament. Moreover, it reeks of purdah, a perfume I do not like. As for being a disappointed spinster, except for moments when I've been dazzled, misled, or dead tired, marriage has not looked tempting. To have attached myself to one man would have obscured my vision of men in general. Any woman who knows one male as mate is not going to know many other men at all except, if she is so inclined, carnally. By staying single I have one saintly virtue as far as men are concerned, even though it is by default: I can't be unfaithful to one of their sex. I am virtuous. Furthermore, I'm experienced. Though I've borne a son, I'm past childbearing. I'm damn near past caring. What safer confidante for any man? I'm more trustworthy even than his mother.

1
LOVE AND EMOTIONS

On paper, some men are magnificently, hugely, poetically emotional, but in spoken Mantalk they seem timid and even dumb, particularly to a woman who is busy pouring out her feelings as fast as they occur. Women are acutely sensitive, so keen to air their feelings, and some of them so eager to inflict them upon others that it may begin to appear in contrast that men have no genuine emotions at all. What are these "feelings" men are denied and women want them to recognize? Feelings of incompleteness, of emotional vulnerability, of boundless tenderness, and of bitter blame. In other words, what it feels like to be a woman.

Where women gather, they discuss, compare, describe emotions the way men do football tactics. Love, jealousy and anger are subjects for kitchen councils, and are always attended by complaint, often by tears. When men gather in groups, it is according to their jobs, or their hobbies, or their common criminality, and their conversation is largely anecdotal, advancing an heroic saga in which the teller himself becomes a performer. Although male conversation can lead to competitive joke telling or filibustering, a man rarely stops the flow of table talk because it concerns something he feels too strongly to talk about, as just the other day in my hearing an intelligent woman stopped a group discussing the psychology of modern Japan because she could not endure the painful memory of that country's behavior during the war. (No wonder it is her husband and not she who invents computer parts. At least, he can bear to face the competition.) I've known men to boast and I've heard them lie; however, I've never seen a heterosexual male sulk because the party wasn't paying enough attention to him, or watched one dominate a roomful of people with tales of his father's cruelty and the miseries of his childhood.

Even in Congress, male conversation doesn't often end with participants never, never speaking to each other again. This does, however, frequently happen among women. To disagree with a female who is glaring, unreflecting, all-feeling, at the center of her own universe, is to become her enemy for life. There aren't many human beings around as bullying as a self-centered, hypersensitive woman, and few so well equipped to practice emotional blackmail. She is armed with rage, sulks, and tears to use against those who do not do as she wants them to, or think as she thinks they should. When feelings rule, an insufficiency of imagination peculiar to babies and some women is displayed; the feeler assumes all existence is dependent upon her opinion of it and has been designed to stroke her, praise her, feed her, make her feel good. Some of our females are nursery-trained to consider themselves source, purpose and judge of all human behavior; they live in a state of persistent bad temper because the opinions they cherish are based on feelings, not knowledge or observation, and are therefore constantly belied by life. The solipsistic woman will serve those who please her because to please her merits reward; by the same token, she shows no mercy to those who displease her. They have earned punishments, the most awful of which is to be deprived of her company. This is the extreme end of feelingness, and there's a lot of it around.

Males, meanwhile, lope out to the playground where they learn to give harder knocks than they get, to delight in the pleasures of physical and intellectual contest, and to run away if they can't be good losers. They learn to influence other men if they can, to follow a leader if they must, and to organize their own rebellion if nothing else is possible. Generally, they are drawn to self-reliance because life is tough, and there is always the chance others will need someone to rely upon. There is a telephone booth in every man's imagination and he fancies that the moment destiny requires it, he can rush in, strip off his city duds, and emerge as Superman in full possession of astonishing powers.

In fact, the male has his feelings even though women do not recognize them, because they are not usually expressed or extroverted; they are protective and used to shield his dearest part, his ego, against real or imagined attack. A man who is disastrously far gone in egotism can become so utterly selfish he hoards all feelings against the demands he believes are made upon him by a high, noble calling. The male ego, when it goes too far, will cut off anyone who does not do it good or improve its image of itself; *in extremis*, it will even cut the man off from himself and try to cut him off from women who are emoting at the top of their lungs and nagging him to listen. This is a rare condition, however, less common than touchy women suppose. Personally, I've known only one man intimately who was padded in egotism like a samurai in armor, and so encased it was hard to tell if anyone was at home. Somebody, probably a woman, must have terrified him very much to make him hide that way. He was an amusing man too, a charmer, and a mischief maker who used human beings as test tubes in his own laboratory. In bed, only his penis was present. I can still remember his well-pitched, actorish voice, even though nothing noteworthy was said.

The difference between the playground imagination of

the male with its brand of egotism and the nursery feelings of the female is the difference between a man I know who, after six flying lessons, dreams of the day he will be able to take over the controls of a jumbo jet when the pilot is stricken by a heart attack, and a woman I know who cannot sleep on airplanes because she feels that if her consciousness lapses (unskilled and ignorant though it is) the plane will go out of control and crash. In a crisis, I'd rather be with the man, though I'd prefer the odds if he were half so competent as he imagines himself to be. Nevertheless, it is rarely said these days that women should try to quiver less in the grip of self-absorbed emotions and achieve austerity of feeling; on the contrary, we keep hearing that men should be more emotional, by which it is meant they should respond to challenge or criticism as brainlessly as many women do.

Tender feelings defend nobody of either sex from cruelty or stupidity. Hitler loved his dog. To overstate the importance of feelings the way women and some men are doing is to open the door to sentimentality. It glorifies all the superficial emotions that prohibit free thought and, perversely, free feelings too, because as soon as specific emotions are licensed, they must be displayed when required, whether they are genuinely felt or not. In reality, no Mantalk exists for many feelings and concepts women find ordinary. Men who try to win approval by speaking these feelings must use an emasculated language, full of holes and solecisms like "meaningful" and "sensitized" and the egregious "personhood," all of them flyspecks on humor and compassion. In some avant-garde circles, males have started to display the vocabulary of sentimentality like tail feathers; their hypersensitivity to babies and puppies, as well as their impassioned feminism, has started to be the same seductive ploy it has always been for women.

Once upon a time, when I was a little girl, my family had a "Victory Garden" in which we grew vegetables for the war effort. It wasn't always easy even for a feeling female child to see the connection. On the home front our enemies were rabbits and my father armed himself with a rifle against their raids on the carrots. Usually he was an excellent marksman who could shoot a bunny through its eye from a considerable distance. One morning, still bleary from sleep, he managed only to wound the marauder. It lay on the lawn moaning in a way I had never imagined a rabbit could. The sound was so heartbreaking, and my unpracticed female heart so eager to be broken, I threw myself over the body of the wounded cottontail to intercept the *coup de grâce*. I ached for the rabbit. It was quite a pleasant feeling. In a frenzy of anthropomorphism, I saw its little pink eyes beseeching me for life. I was that bunny's last chance. My younger brother was vastly amused, and my father was so charmed he spent a long time, though not normally a patient man, explaining to me, while the rabbit suffered, the real cruelty and stupidity of my feelings.

"We can't live in a world swarming with rabbits and have enough for children to eat too," he said.

"Why can't you make enough food for everyone?" I cried, assigning him, the male, responsibility for my feelings and blaming him for injustice. "It's not fair. Why don't you make enough for children and rabbits too?"

"It's not I who am not fair," my father said. "It's the rabbit who overeats."

To be as sensitive as a feeling woman is easy, too easy. It can fascinate without information, dominate without wit, bully without substance, excuse cruelty and laziness, and in the end require others to do all its dirty work. It wouldn't profit either sex if men sacrificed their broadness of view to the pinhole vision of a hypersensitive woman. In a book called *The New Male*, "from macho to sensitive but still all male," Herb Goldberg, an American described, courageously, by his publishers as "the most important voice in male liberation today," talks about "gender fantasy which perpetuates the annihilation of each other's full personhood," and he thinks men, in order to keep power (he doesn't say how they got it in the first place), have perpetuated this "fantasy" and become its victims. Deplorable "personhood" to one side, gender is not a fantasy. It exists. They exist. This seems a basic point, just as it does that genders must engender differences of all kinds, including the way people feel; however, it didn't seem basic recently to a feminist interviewer who asked me in a very intense, feeling, and opinionated tone, in what way, what single way, I dared suppose there existed one real, major difference between the sexes?

"We can be mothers . . ." I began.

"Are you trying to tell me," she interrupted, too angry to hear me out, "that maternity is sex-linked?"

Lots of things are sex-linked. The male unconscious and subconscious and his consciousness too are subject to different emphases, anxieties, experiences and ambitions. How can his feelings be the same as a woman's? Why should he respond emotionally as much or as often or the same way women do? Why, for example, should men cry? There's no special virtue in tears. Women cry more than enough for both sexes and oceans more than compassion requires. It's self-pity that makes the greatest demands on those tiny glands at the corners of our eyes. All men hate a woman's tears and turn away from them not out of coldness, as weeping women believe, but because tears make men helpless, tears defeat freedom, tears embarrass justice. When a woman is crying, a man is left only two choices: to give in to whatever demands she makes, no matter how they outrage his own feelings, so she'll stop; or to storm out, slam the door, and suffer his guilt alone. Though men are bombastic and pompous in defense of their egos, they do not generally like a histrionic display of driven, high-pitched feelings reaching a top note beyond human endurance or control. The faster a female moves into this mode, which comes easily to most women, the faster he retreats; or the more likely he will roar and swing his paw like a lion stung to anger by a wasp. Then, she finds him unfeeling. Toward the terrifying end of love, I've been gripped myself by a tantrum on the edge of hysteria that many women I know call "trying to get through to him." The men have fled in understandable confusion and rage.

It's a breeze to cry. Babies do it all the time, and both sexes find themselves moved at displays of great kindness and enraged by inhumanity. Some terrors, however, emerge only in nightmares and some desires are as strong as awe, too strong for words. When men have deep emotions it often happens, as it does less often to women, that the greater their emotion, the quieter they become. Some chew over their reactions, some are shaken to the core by them, and some are thinking how to translate them into action or work. For the many males who function in reality, or even in their imaginations, at the extreme edge of safety or sanity, failure can be the death not only of them, but also of those who depend upon them, and they have no time to fiddle with feelings. "Bottle" is everything, and a man who drops his to wipe his eyes is a danger to everyone. Some men function because of their fear, not in spite of it. They do what they fear doing because they are driven by a greater fear of failing to have done it. Courage, heroic longings, love of freedom, ambition and terror of failing, are feelings too, whether spoken or not. Even though they can do harm, they are also a vital component in human survival that has saved us all in the past and may be needed to save us again. These brave, grave feelings have been lumped together as "machismo," a designation for the male's overstatement just as "hysteria" is for the female's. "Machismo" has been getting a bad press recently because it can be exploited on a grand scale; nevertheless, it must be the exploitation of feelings that is invidious, not the feelings themselves. My own experience of pure machismo is small. I met it once in Vietnam.

I have never been able to remember the order of military ranks, or to recognize their insignia, though I know they are very important to men. The man of machismo I knew was, I think, a sergeant major in the American army; whatever it was, he had achieved the highest rank a common soldier can and it brought much glitter to his tunic. I had been in Southeast Asia for about a month near the end of the war, doing my best to attract no attention. I daresay I was the only person for miles around without an ax to grind. Being a generally right-thinking individual, I disapproved of the American presence; certainly, I preferred the bars in Saigon patronized by right-thinking Westerners. My specific interest was not political. Males collect in great numbers around a war zone and I thought I could observe them there in a way few women of my generation born in the United States have been able to do. As I pored over maps with my journalist colleagues I wasn't as interested in the next offensive battle as I was in the trembling excitement of even the most pot-bellied, chain-smoking, hard-drinking, adulterous hack at finding himself so close to the clash of good with evil. Somewhere in that primal tumult, if male emotions were ever to be in evidence, I figured they would have to make themselves known. On a chessboard where the pawns were armed with bazookas, where hesitation was subversive, and where high seriousness justified uninhibited debauchery, I expected to learn more about male pride. (Years later in London, I was coming out of a cinema where I had just seen a black comedy about war when I bumped into a celebrated photojournalist I had known in Saigon.

("You were laughing!" he thundered. "How could you laugh?"

(Oddly, these were the very words used decades before by the Frenchman who deflowered me.)

The sergeant major met me at the front desk of the Grand Hotel. He was in his late fifties I guessed, though soldiers are like monks and habitual prisoners in that they often look much younger than they are. He was tall and lanky, in the stretched, rubbery American way. The hollow of his throat was puckered by a scar that disappeared under his collar. Men can be made attractive by scars that would ruin a woman.

"A gift from the Japanese," he said, when he saw me notice it, "in the 'Big One.' "

I liked the way he said "Big One"; it sounded corn-fed, safe, old-fashioned. He spoke with a southern drawl too, so his invitation to dinner was naturally courteous to my northern ear. When he told me it had been a long time since he'd talked to "an American lady," I knew he was a man to take bar girls as his due, but to treat me like a hometown princess. (Unless he found out I was a Jew from the big city, in which case I would just have to outwit him. I've never met a soldier free from racial prejudice of one sort or another.) In short, I said yes to dinner.

We were the only customers on the broad dining terrace of the hotel. Motor scooters were buzzing home before darkness fell on potholes and other hazards. He told me his name and his rank too. I told him I was a journalist. This alarmed him. He probably saw it as a bid for butch courage. Engaging though courage is in both sexes, it is not the same for them; the truly brave female isn't the one who swans around a battlefield with her Pentax, it's she who outpoints her lover at a game of tennis.

Apparently the sergeant major was not one of those men attracted to a pert imitation of his own kind of bravery; maybe he even had an idea of how much harder it is for a woman to find the courage required by her own kind of fear. When I said vaguely, "Features, you know, human interest," he relaxed. He came from Georgia, he told me, and was amused when I asked if that created difficulties with the southern blacks under his command.

"It's only ever been the enemy gives me trouble," he said.

I had been to Georgia a few times in my childhood so I dredged up what I could, though it wasn't much: suburbs without pavements, an outsize moon, Spanish moss like ectoplasm around the trees it has killed.

"Yes, ma'am," he said, "that's Georgia. That's my Georgia."

Our aged waiter knew a hero when he saw one, so he put the bottle of bourbon on our table with the food and left it to its fate while he went to smoke with the kitchen staff. The sergeant major told me about his mother, a countrywoman who distilled her own whiskey; and he said he'd had a wife once. "I don't blame her for leaving me," he said. "A career soldier's no kind of husband." His voice was steady, his words without apparent feeling. To my surprise, however, for I too had the prejudice against warriors just coming into fashion, I started to know I was in the presence of a lonely, powerful emotion that was not struggling to express itself, the way mine always does; rather it was trying to accept itself. We talked a little more about home, or at least he did; I listened. Then, he turned his head and looked out at the dark streets in a reverie so bleak and deep it was hard not to tumble into it with him.

I was very tired, it so happened, and open to impressions. I had just returned from a foray on the Mekong River where for the first time I had listened to the sound of men in battle; it's like the rumble of an avalanche, or an earthquake: an organic planetary disturbance beyond prayers or human will. My Vietnamese guide, standing beside me, described the weapon responsible for each explosion and told me how much the ammunition cost. He was a Catholic with ten children, and he said that for the price of one small flash we could see on the horizon he could have fed his family for a month or more. I looked at the sergeant major who was silent, pondering, and I wondered if he knew he was a purveyor of hunger to Catholic kiddies? Probably not. He had sums of his own to make out of the explosions.

The night was dead quiet. The sergeant major was motionless, except when he raised his glass. Even the hotel cat barely twitched his ear at the scurry of small nails under a neighboring table. Surreptitiously, I glanced at my watch.

"I had a brother," the sergeant major said after a while. He turned to face me. He looked puzzled. "Kid brother. Wanted to be a soldier like me. Idolized me. Then he goes and gets himself killed in a motorcycle accident. Coming home from his girlfriend's house. Don't that take the biscuit?" He turned the glass in his hand.

I wondered if this was it at last? Was this why he wanted to talk to an "American lady"? Was his brother's death the reason for the exhausting emotional force I felt from the taciturn, probably not awfully bright, old soldier?

"I'm sorry," I said. "That's a terrible thing."

"They happen. They happen," he said.

He moved his hand off the table between us because he was afraid I was about to touch it in sympathy and that was not at all what he wanted. I lit a cigarette and blew the smoke toward an insect circling our table, so the sergeant major would know I wasn't watching him with pity, or threatening to unman him. He was a skittish creature, deep down. I wondered what the bar girls made of him: a quick, functional screw, I imagined, grateful, and then immediately alone again.

"Fact is," he said, "I'm perplexed."

For once, I held my tongue and did not try to make an inarticulate man say what I meant.

"I know even the Japs had mothers," he said. "That didn't stop them doing wrong. Real wrong. Like in the Bible. I knew what I had to do that time. Always known that. Now, you take this one? Hell!"

"Hell" could have been an epithet or a description.

"This one. My men ask me, 'Sergeant major, what are we doing here?' They shouldn't ought to have to ask me. I just do not know."

He was struggling. I wanted to do something for him. What could I do? I was no bar girl and he filled his own glass, so I waited.

"I've never asked what I was doing there. That's something I've known. I could comfort men when they'd had their legs blown off, and when they were dying. There's a lot of things worse than dying. Trouble is, I've forgotten what they are. What are they?"

He reached for the bottle again.

"I'm starting to seriously wonder," he said.

Three young soldiers stepped out of the darkness. One of them was black, and looked as worried as the mother of an ailing child. Gently, with ceremony quite like tenderness, he helped the sergeant major to his feet while his companions gathered up hat, cigarettes, wallet. One of the soldiers counted out money for our bill. As they walked away the sergeant major said, "Gentlemen, I do not know. I just don't know."

"Yessir," they answered together.

My old soldier was caught on the turn, just another employee at retirement age. His place was already being taken by the new popular hero who shows feelings of the feminine variety. Not long ago, for example, a science-fiction television series gave us a protagonist who put the entire planet Earth at risk in order to rescue his girlfriend from fiendish aliens. No sergeant major would have dreamed of endangering his people for his doxy, or turning our epic into a soap opera. The old warrior is now being called an absurd archetype and a chauvinistic invention, which is as may be; yet, along with him go physical courage, highmindedness, adventurous curiosity, fidelity to a cause, and other valid male feelings that happen also to require freedom from the hearthside and the romance of women.

Romantic love is not a feminine invention; on the contrary, the free male is a high-flying romantic, not pragmatic in love at all, sometimes able to express himself in excited Mantalk, along the lines of:

> Till a' the seas gang dry, my dear,
> And the rocks melt wi' the sun;
> I will luve thee still, my dear,
> While the sands o' life shall run.

Unfortunately, the male's romance is deadly to the female. He doesn't want to share lifelong bliss in a cottage, or punctuate ecstasy with three hot meals and Christmas at his in-laws; that's not the male's idea of romance, or the way he dreams love will be. For a man, romantic love is worship. He doesn't want to do great things with a woman, he wants to do them for her. Even the knight who rescued his princess from bondage didn't need the princess any more than he needed the dragon. Worship is love from a safe distance. Out of its emotional power men have written the greatest romantic poetry in all languages, and the crudest pornography. These are both forms that abstract love and detach the author from the demanding, reforming, feeling, predatory female. The worshiping male wants the female to keep her mystery and apartness; he wants her to observe how wonderful he is, how free. He wants her to applaud his power and even to be freed by it herself, but he does not want her to come too close, to clip his wings, or threaten him with mortal failure.

Like any other woman, I used to believe I could, or even should, reform a man. Isn't that what maleness from its very boyhood asks women to do? A woman wants a man to make her happy, and doesn't a man dare each new woman to make him good? However, to be happy and to be good have only one thing in common: they are both conditions free from longing. Because the worldly ambitions of a woman are attenuated while her expectations of love are specific, it is easier for her to imagine that romantic happiness will last than it is for a man to believe he can be good for the rest of his life. He has never, anyway, expected the woman he adores to make him good. Where did she ever get that idea? He has expected her to make him feel good, and that is not the same thing at all. He does not want to be reformed. On the contrary, he wants his goddess to accept him utterly, to forgive him, and to absolve him from guilt. If she considers that his being good is primarily a matter of making her happy, and that making her happy means he must never want anyone else again or anything at all except what she wants too, then the man struggles under a great burden. The celestial beauty for whom he hoped to lasso stars and planets appears only to want a slave who will obey her house rules and assume absolute responsibility for her emotional well-being. This was not the job he applied for when he entered her temple.

I have a friend who is a successful businesswoman; she is a statuesque spinster in her mid-forties, and she has never wanted to marry. On a holiday abroad she met a handsome, older man who was celebrating his divorce, and they had a lighthearted affair. When they returned, she was surprised that his courtship continued; he was persistent, thoughtful, witty and adoring. She started to feel very happy.

"He said he was 'weak,'" she told me once when their affair was still fresh. "What does a man mean when he says that?"

It so happens when a man says he is weak, in Mantalk it means that, first, he will be unfaithful and, then, he will be unable to bear his guilt without making the woman suffer too.

"It's a warning," I told her.

She laughed.

"Don't be silly," she said. Her salesmen and board of directors would have been amazed to see her blush. "He says I'm the best woman he's met in twenty years. He idolizes me. He approves of me. I can make him strong."

When women are happy in love their old friends don't see much of them, and for a few months I heard no more. The next time we met, she was sad and confused. Her lover had decamped abruptly. After whispering love and marriage until she was besotted, he had left her high and dry on the pedestal he had built.

"As soon as I began to think it might work between us in spite of all the discrepancies of income and prestige, it was as though I'd given him a license to lie to me, betray me, and embarrass me," she said. "Now he's back with someone he knew before me. Someone younger who, I daresay, doesn't mind when he calls her 'a girl,' which used to make me feel belittled and silly. Why?"

Maybe he was afraid he wasn't good enough to make a clever woman happy. Maybe he had hoped she would not take him as a serious contender for a position she had never advertised. Maybe he was a man who preferred to worship from a melancholy distance. Maybe he required a more conventional goddess. Maybe he was a common rogue. Instead of the agent of his reform, my friend became the agent of his guilt, and he of her unhappiness, as often happens when a vain, curious man blows carelessly on the vestal embers.

After an affair I had with an admiring, reverential lover was over, we met once for lunch and during the ensuing postmortem I mentioned to him early occasions when our lovemaking, which had gone off toward the end, had been spectacular. Now, this man was truly gifted for crossword puzzles; he used big words with precision, albeit usually only one at a time.

"Simulacrum," he said to me, "you were being a simulacrum."

"Not silk, just dacron?" I thought, and sipped some bitter wine.

We let the issue drop with considerable relief on both sides; we dropped each other too. Later, when I was cool, I started to see what he meant, or at least what he had said, and how it pertained to the subject of male worship. A simulacrum is a mere image of a great abstract; for a Catholic like him it was a sort of roadside altar, a paltry symbol for divinity offering the chance for a moment of adoration on the hoof. Under those circumstances I could of course have been the simulacrum for another, mightier woman. Or perhaps a simulacrum for all-cunt. Most men never love a woman for herself; they worship her for the comfort she gives them, or for a part she has in common with the great divine. To abandon the little heaps on the verge as soon as they threaten an upkeep more particular is mean, but not many men are generous by inclination.

Women are not endowed for worship. It is too ecstatic and too mysterious to suit the cosy feminine romance. Although a woman does not worship her man for what he has in common with all men, she needs to respect something about him that can be seen as his special strength. Three quarters of the married women who complain of loss of sexual interest in their prosperous, kindly husbands are suffering from loss of respect. Respect is never inexplicable; it always has its reasons. Sometimes the female's drive to respect assumes all the folly and fury of masochism, so that if there is nothing else to respect she'll settle for his left hook. I knew girls at school who respected men for the cars they drove and were proud to be seen in the passenger's seat. Respect is an aphrodisiac for the female and whether the cause is genetic common sense or frivolity, the concomitant of respect is obedience. The indisputable evidence of the female's desire to respect her mate and the obedience this implicitly entails create a puzzle for egalitarians. One solution is to overstate the tenderness and wisdom of women while deriding male talents, calling them a "myth" and making men out to be power-mad brutes; this logically means women should respect, obey, and fall in love with each other which, in some smart circles, they have been doing. A considerable amount of extreme feminism has been an apology for lesbianism. Feminists who have not quite mustered the courage of their convictions and still need to live with men of their own have found another way to solve the respect/obedience/equality conundrum. They bully their personal males into agreeing with everything they say and do, so they can then say and do as they please without argument and call it obedience, or at least agreement. There can be no other reason why intelligent middle-class men, always the most hagridden, sit at their own tables nodding their heads at outlandish theories: that marital sex is rape, for instance; that only male prejudice prevents women from equal control of the world; that females are in every way as strong, as ambitious, as intellectual as the men these very females are longing to respect and rarely do for agreeing with them, or even for worshiping them.

A man and a woman have one important thing in common at the start of a romance: they are both in love with him. Her highly strung feelings tell her this is the man, the only man, the predestined mate with whom her fulfillment will be achieved. Love makes women very superstitious. Witches used to do most of their trade in love potions. Marriage counselors and advice columnists are supposed to provide them now. Love makes women incautious and forgetful of past love; and love makes women unethical, because for them it transcends everything. (Lust does similar things to men, though, mercifully, it's much more quickly over.) He, in the meantime, feels quite a fellow to have found himself such a neat pocket goddess. He loves the way she makes him feel: heroic, strong, young, gifted, protective, and ready for any grand deeds she may require. If they are both older, handicapped, unattractive, or terrified of being alone, they both think "this is the best I can do," in which case their union has a good chance of success. Yet, new lovers don't precisely "think" anything at all because their senses are so excited at the prospect of gratification that what goes on in the heads of two people gripped by such turmoil can hardly be described as "thought." They "sense" it, or maybe they smell it, or perhaps they just "come up with it."

The man and woman in love know they are doing something wonderful, and so they are; the trouble is, each is doing it with someone who is doing something else. In her mind, and maybe in her very cells, is the great good she was born for: the rational, urgent, practical good of cupboards, roast meat, fire and shelter, and of offspring. The only deed she really requires of her hero is to come off his high horse and settle down. She is interior decorating the future; he, at the same time, is altogether in the present. The very sight of her and he forgets to do all those ordinary things that everyone ought to do, like mind his step, and read the road ahead. He's dancing in the dark, and it feels great. He'll stop when the tune ends.

All her cunning is engaged in the game and cunning is so busy making a plot it fails to see what's happening in front of its bedroom eyes. Willingly, she abandons her friends and her old pursuits to undertake contortions of personality, taste and physique, briefly painful for her perhaps, while serving to enhance the vision he holds of himself as quite a lad. At every newsstand there are thousands of glossy pages, richly illustrated, instructing her how to act, feel, look, to get her man or keep him. The strange adjustment of the courting female to her dreamboat's ego is as much nature as it is guile. She is making believe, and she really means it. When the affair goes wrong, she will lie awake at night wondering what she did wrong. Which was her false move? What should she have done differently?

Not so long ago, the only lure a female needed for her line was virginity. Her mother, or her mother's mother, used to warn her that no man wanted to have and hold what he'd already had and held in the backseat of his car. Granny's lesson went home to the heart of the female. The generation of women liberated into promiscuity cannot forget that a man tires of sex with the same partner, and at the same time they believe nobody tires of love; so only if sex is love, are all cakes made to have and eat. A woman will try to use sex as she once used the withholding of it: to bind a man into the game nature plays. She'll design herself after his favorite sexual icon in black leather or dimity skirts. If he wants to make love in a telephone booth or on the bed he shares with his legal mate, she'll play along. She'll even like it, if it pleases him. At least, she'll try to like it until she has him fast, and after she's had his child she'll probably be unable to go on trying. She'll do her best to hide her fear that he is going to want another female, and she will slowly tie him up in guilt.

Unfeeling though men are supposed to be, they are highly susceptible to guilt, partly because they are regularly accused of having no feelings at all, a crime worthy of a life sentence. Because a man is never so sure of his preeminence in bed as he wants to be, he is also sensitive to sexual jealousy, and some women, in pursuit of the utter rightness of the union they foresee, feel justified in using that dreadful weapon to ensnare him. For his own good, of course. I once was asked by a women's magazine to write a piece advising readers on ways to raise the green devil and torture their recalcitrant men into submission. I could have used the money, but I do have a conscience after all, and I turned the piece down. A man wrote it instead.

So, there is young Romeo splashing around in a warm, scented bath and sure he can pull the plug when the time comes. Any other male in nature would at this point gather some reeds, make a nest, help create progeny, and in due course move on to the next amorous adventure. However, the human male is burdened with guilt, vows, mortgages, the romance of women, and offspring who take an unconscionable time to grow up. Gradually, it begins to dawn on the man in love that he is no longer a free agent. The tail is off his kite. The ship is sailing without him. Another man is walking on the moon, and in personal, private ways his territory has been invaded. Without his knowing precisely how it happened, he has become the source of another person's happiness and expectations; thus, overnight it seems, he has become a potential agent of her disappointment and misery. While the hunter was momentarily distracted by his reflection in a flattering pool, the gazelle turned into a love-starved tigress. His only choices are to do the "right" thing and be a husband (at least, a live-in lover—trendy euphemism, as women see it, for a "fiancé"), or do the "wrong" thing and be a rat.

The vanity that entraps the male initially can serve to disentangle him at that crucial moment in an affair when he submits—or doesn't. He measures the idea of himself as a rat against the idea of himself as a monogamous mate; he measures his guilt or even his weariness against his delight in freedom. Although neither image is alluring, it's easier to get over feeling like a rat than feeling like a husband, so many men at this point cut loose and run without stumbling. Women wonder why it so often happens that a man who has been played unsuccessfully on the line for years will suddenly break free and then, within days, blissfully commit himself to a blonde he bumped into at the supermarket.

This occurs for several reasons: first, he glimpsed at the center of the hurricane he is fleeing a real serenity, and that is something the blonde in the frozen-foods section notices right away and adapts herself to flatter. Second, he may be celebrating in riproaring style his release from what had begun to feel like servitude, and he goes too far. Finally, he needs a swift bulwark against any temptation to return out of guilt, or even out of love, to the female he made unhappy. He is protecting himself, his freedom, his infallibility, against blackmail, and he's so busy looking over his shoulder he does not notice there is another hungry tigress in his path.

Even if he loved the woman from whom he fled, and is melancholy for a while, his involvement is unlikely to have contained the same investment as hers. Relationship is her vocation, rarely his. And it is her prelude to forever. Furthermore, while he can go on and on seducing and being seduced, she never knows which man is the last she will be able to pull. So, when a lover decamps, he takes all future with him and leaves a vacuum that for a while defies philosophy, music and joy. No doubt there are women who can backpedal on love, but my impression, and that of every female I know, is that the woman's heart mends slowly and the torch was invented for her to carry.

"The male's need to love is just as strong as the female's," a man friend said. "Only his fear is much greater."

"Fear of what?" I asked.

"Of being mistaken," he said.

"In her, or by her?"

"Both," my friend said.

A woman's fear is less because once in love she figures she—and love, of course—will change any little things about the man (his alcoholism, say, his drug addiction, his homosexuality, his temper, his fecklessness) that could threaten the utter rightness of their union and its inexorable practicality, its complete uniqueness, its incontrovertible feasibility. She does all she can to assuage his fears and let him know he cannot live without her as his very own embodiment of everything he worships in the female. He, in the meantime, is thinking she has great legs. In short, the male, who falls in love with the message, never knows the messenger; the female falls in love with the messenger and doesn't listen to a word he's saying.

_2_
SEX

When it comes to sex, and everything else, the male's great fear is of failure, and the female's is of not being loved. For a man, sex is always to some degree an edgy performance, more ritual than romance, a sport with conscience as an indulgent referee. Plain, unadulterated fucking is maleish and quite a few men manage to pull the deed off; very few men, however, in feminine estimation are better than boring lovers. Because possible failure haunts men and because their erections are vulnerable to the racket of consciousness as well as to the whimpers of the subconscious, they can be grimly determined in bed, and determination is not voluptuous; they are competitive too, and their moments of climax and dominance are often achieved without tact or sensuousness. By feminine standards, which happen to be the lovemaking standards of the moment, most men are lousy lovers; however, feminine standards are also those of a daydream or, worse, the standards of their favorite romantic fiction:

> Then, like a tidal wave sweeping everything before it, longing claimed her utterly. She became alive beneath his hands . . . he uttered an anguished cry and buried his face in the perfumed softness of her breasts. . . . Together they climbed to

34

devastating heights until they were consumed simultaneously
by a flood of fire which completely overwhelmed them. . . .
"I love you," she murmured. . . .
"And I love you," he murmured huskily. . . .
                    (*The Odds Against* by Margaret Pargeter,
                                        Harlequin, 1984.)

What chance has a real man against that kind of sexual
fantasy? A real woman is only going to approach comparable ecstasy when she imagines herself in love. Because her
need to love and be loved is smoldering and constant as a
vestal fire, the young female is more randy than the male,
whose lust rises or falls according to what is on offer. In
the exhaustive *Hite Report on Male Sexuality*, it is concluded
that sexual intercourse for men is satisfying not merely because of emotional attachment to the beloved, "but also
from the deeply engraved cultural meaning of the act.
Through intercourse a man participates in the cultural symbolism of patriarchy and gains a sense of belonging to society
with the status/identity of 'male.' " (*The Hite Report on Male
Sexuality* by Shere Hite, New York, Knopf, 1981.)
    In the equally exhaustive *Hite Report* on Female Sexuality,
one woman, when asked if she liked intercourse, replied in
words I see over and over again in letters from the lovelorn
and love-torn: "I don't know—on the one hand, I wouldn't
like intercourse at all probably if I didn't love him. By itself,
intercourse is really nothing, but with him on the other end,
it's dynamite. . . ." (*The Hite Report* by Shere Hite, New
York, Macmillan, 1976.) Hite goes on to say in her conclusion to the book on women, "Intercourse, as a pleasur-
able form of physical contact, will always be one of the
ways people choose to relate. . . ."
    True enough, I guess. However, relate to what? Not, it
seems, to each other. When a man screws, he screws himself
into "Cultural Symbolism," while his partner is making

love to love or she isn't that crazy about the whole idea. Sex has become love for her, more than ever now that she is freed from unwanted pregnancy. Intercourse is a female relating passionately to the man in her arms; he, however, at moments of greatest intensity is relating passionately to himself. Fucking is a celebration of the male's vigor and briefly it relieves him of his fear of failing. It has been generous of women to put up with it, though heaven knows many of them do it without complaint only when they are in love.

Naturally, women think their own loving, languorous way of sex is better, and so it is . . . for them. Recently, they have been trying to bully and shame men into thinking it would be better for them too, though the truth is it would be less demanding, enslaving, perplexing and strenuous for a healthy male to screw a thousand women in his lifetime than to try to please one, and the potential for failure would be less. A man without the least skill for sensuous love-making has as satisfying a love life as any other man and no shortage of acquiescent partners. He can get laid as often as a sensitive or gymnastic lover and, as far as he is concerned, just as well. Being a rapid, brutish lover or a slow, timid one does not prevent his success in the world of business and action; on the contrary, it may help him there by concentrating his energy and imagination. Plenty of female partners are always ready, even eager, to put up with ineptitude in bed as long as the male is a good provider and free from repellent habits. In my own experience, a great uninhibited lover is, anyhow, very like a great ballroom dancer: good at what he's good at, and hard to take seriously at anything else. Inventive love-making is similar to any other form of charm—a little goes a long way, and when it has gone its way, there's not much left.

Perhaps the human male is designed by nature to be less sensuous than the female so that he doesn't waste time lolling around the hearth fire instead of penetrating and impregnating as many partners as possible while he's in his prime, the way many other animals do. And possibly the female is more sensuous so that she doesn't become restless while pregnant or while the men are away; she is easily pleasured, in fact, and not necessarily by a man. Sensuousness is a pastime of the harem that goes with silks and chocolates and eunuchs in attendance. The trail of fingers over skin is a purring nursery delight, a leisurely kind of human grooming, very different from the explosive uniting of sex organs.

Many women say they are capable of two kinds of orgasm, one slow and syrupy, the other blazing during intercourse; even more women say they have never known the second, and are only capable of the first. Now that reproduction has become a concern only after love, and certainly after being loved, maleish wham-bam seems superfluous and even offensive to the pleasure-seeking "new woman." Most men are good fellows who would honestly rather give pleasure to their partners than not, if only out of vanity. The new sexual chivalry, however, threatens the male with the dreaded old failure to get it up, and also with failure to keep it up for the long process of his partner's excitement, as well as failure to please even when he does.

Suddenly, it's no longer altogether normal or fair for a man to fuck like a man, and he's likely to be scolded for it if he insists upon his way, or if he knows no other way, or if there is no other way, or if he is reluctant to make love in an unmanly way because—whatever trendy folk advocate—he really does not want to be effeminate, least of all in bed. He is being asked, and not always sweetly, by sexologists, therapists, advice columnists, and his partners, to risk failure so that women can feel well and truly loved. What does he get in return for his courage and industry? The satisfaction of pleasing her, which is in its way a kind of slavery. One fear is being traded off against another, hers against his. By requiring the male to be sensuous, even demanding it, the female is ordering him to do her a favor. Making love is her metaphor for true love, entailing commitment as well as sometimes an hour of foreplay, and she intends it should be his too. However, the moment a man agrees to make love with his fingertips instead of his cock, he is sharpening the shears for Delilah, and he knows he can't trust her not to use them.

Recently, I watched a film on television about psychosexual counseling. It was made around a middle-aged couple who had volunteered to speak publicly of the improvement in their sex lives after "working" for a year with a therapist. Although people who want to tell their intimate secrets to the world may not be typical of the majority, thanks to our insatiable appetite for confession in aid of universal soul searching, they are endowed with specious veracity, and an audience is more inclined to believe them than its own experience.

"On behalf of the viewers I want to thank this couple for agreeing to talk to us," said the female sex therapist, though this viewer at least was tempted to ring the station and say not all of us were grateful; a lot of us were prurient. Wife and husband dutifully told us how their lovemaking had improved when he, after fifteen years of what he thought was normal marital sex, had been dragged off to a therapist who instructed him to stop screwing his wife; just to hold her, stroke her, tickle her, for days, weeks even, until she said she was ready for the simple deed to which we all owe our conception. Never had I seen two such miserable people. She, frowning and chain-smoking, told us how much happier her marriage had become now that her husband was "sensitized" to her needs. He, poor old dear, sat with hanging head, now and again smiling sheepishly at the camera that was recording his humiliation for all the neighbors and his fellows at work. He was a picture of dejection. Whatever "improved sex" means, it could hardly be worth so much human misery.

"I think everyone acknowledges these days that women have a right to pleasure, too," said the therapist.

Who assigns such a "right," I wondered? The therapist didn't tell us that, though she certainly made it clear that when the right is not fulfilled, it's the male who must, as usual, take responsibility for the female's lack of pleasure. She put paid to the heroic dream of a female who accepts his lust and gusto and calls it a good time. That, she relegated tacitly to pornography.

Pornography is written by men and for men. It is the literature of male fantasy and ideal, just the way romantic novels are for women. *Nurse Emma's Clinic* is the porn of emission and Harlequin's *The Odds Against* is the porn of omission. The reader of the first comes, and the reader of the second yearns. Both are the literature of self-indulgence and are openly sold in every society that also goes in for psychotherapists and takeout foods. Every male in our communities has recourse to pornography at one time or another, which is why to prove that porn causes men to commit sexual offenses is turning out to be as hard as it would be to prove shaving does. A good friend of mine collects pornography, and he has allowed me free run of his library (trusting of him, too, as he says the pilfering is phenomenal). Pornography expresses the heroic dream of sexual infallibility, and helps the male achieve a semblance of it. A man absorbed in a piece of porn doesn't intend to read, look at, or watch; he intends to masturbate. Porn is altogether pragmatic. It exists to stimulate and satisfy an appetite just the way cook books do, except the porn reader always has his ingredients to hand.

It has been twenty years or so since I first saw a blue movie and began to understand the thrust of porn and how it helps the fears of men. A mysterious Indian gentleman one day walked in off the streets of London to a magazine office where I was working at the time, and announced that if a journalist and photographer would come with him to

Iran he would guarantee an interview with the then shah. What was more, he himself would provide first-class air tickets and accommodation at the finest hotel in Tehran.

"Who, what, where, when?" asked our fearless editor, but never "Why?"

Five days after the photographer and I had been installed in our luxurious hotel, we were still waiting for our promised interview; and we were starting to worry. Our passports had disappeared into the Gucci dispatch case of our guide, who turned out to be not a resident of the country, or even of the planet for all we could tell. Though he was not staying with us, he made regular appearances to announce with decreasing effect that all was going splendidly. To pass time, we bought trinkets in the suqs and swam in the hotel pool (females were still permitted to share an Islamic pool with men in those days). Time passed pleasantly enough except that, unlikely though it may sound, free-lance writers actually need to work for financial and psychological reasons, and the only job offered either of us was to take pictures at the fifth birthday party of the son of one of our guide's "very important contacts." This commission depressed the photographer badly. Every evening, he and I were taken for drinks to the home of one dignitary or another, and, because we had been warned never to so much as whisper "shahinshah," or hint at our project, we found ourselves over and over again in splendid drawing rooms making small talk with handsome men who were obviously as puzzled as we, while servants circled on tiptoe carrying caviar and fly whisks.

One morning, our mysterious guide arrived at the hotel early, and so puffed with import he seemed almost as tall as I was. He said we were that very afternoon to be introduced to the most important personage we had met so far in Persia and maybe, he added in a hushed voice, in our entire lifetimes; a giant among men whose name was not to be spoken, yet whose power was so great our man trembled with excitement at the thought of it. Naturally, we assumed we were at last to meet the shah, and all our strictly non-kosher champagne parties had been vetting trials to make sure we wouldn't spit on the imperial floor, or take an awkward political stand there. I dressed with particular care, and rehearsed all the questions I had prepared, until, at precisely four that afternoon, a big, black limousine arrived to take us to our rendezvous. We drove out of Tehran for several miles to a beautiful house set in a landscaped park. To my despair, however, I saw right away that despite the opulence of the place there were no guards or gun towers; clearly it could not be the residence of a beloved monarch. My heart burned at the prospect of more fish eggs.

We entered a high, domed hall built around an enameled fountain. From one of the distant rooms came the sound of children's laughter, and a woman, scolding. A servant led us through many corridors and small, cloistered gardens into what any American would recognize immediately as a "rumpus room." There were tables laid for card games, Ping-Pong, chess; the walls were paneled in bamboo (wood of good sports everywhere), and a well-stocked bar was being manned by a uniformed servant at the far end of the room. The moment we entered, seven Indians, all in suits and turbans, all of the same placid rotundity as our guide, who was among them, rose from small chintz-colored sofas drawn into a semicircle in the middle of the room. I sat down, as invited with great courtesy. The men sat down. I smiled at the men. The men smiled at me. Could they be a corporate "very important personage"? Did one of them have insignia of high office hidden under his turban? We made the usual small talk: yes, the weather was magnificent; no, I did not find local food too highly spiced; yes, the dowry system was an anachronism, nevertheless, yes, of course I saw the point of it. Servants entered with cold beer

and potato chips instead of caviar, and immediately the pro-
ceedings took on a slightly conspiratorial air. Clearly, we
were waiting. For what? For whom? The men exchanged
glances and nods.

"Now then! Now then!" said our guide, after a while.

"Now then," murmured his replicas.

He rubbed his hands. They rubbed their hands. Someone
must have pushed a button; a screen dropped from the ceil-
ing in full view of where we all sat.

"Give us strength!" I whispered to the photographer, for
I assumed we were about to be subjected to another film of
the shah teaching blind children to read. Then, the curtains
were drawn, a beam of light from a projector set into the
wall behind us passed over the turbaned heads, there was
the hum of machinery, and the words "A Milkman's Morning" appeared in black and white before us. Suddenly, our
little band found itself in what seemed to be a suburban
English kitchen of the 1950s. A jar of marmalade was on
the table, a geranium was wilting on the window ledge; at
the same time I heard peacocks squabbling in our Persian
garden and not a mile away the sun was baking lapis lazuli.
The camera pulled back to show us an English housewife
with platinum hair. She was wearing stiletto heels, and
washing a tea mug. She appeared to be singing. Her chest
swelled. The door flew open, and there stood the milkman,
all in white, a "pinta" in his paw. There was no soundtrack.

"What will you have today?" flashed on the screen.

The question was rhetorical. Within moments, clothes
were strewn everywhere and the housewife was bent over
her kitchen table. The real room, the one in which I sat,
was so still I heard the crunch of a potato chip between
golden teeth on my left.

"Oh, oh, oh, give me what I want!" said the housewife.

The camera zoomed in on sex organs pump-pumping like
parts of a well-oiled machine.

"Take me, take me!" said the housewife.

I didn't know whether I wanted to laugh out of embarrassment, or because the comment was so magnificently redundant.

The milkman had pimples on his rear; his penis, however, was of such mighty proportions the actor must have been he whom I later heard referred to in pornographic circles as "King Dong." Had I been a male, the challenge of an engine like his would have kept my fly forever zipped, but an audible increase in breathing from the darkness around me indicated it was not having this effect on my companions. I was disappointed. I would have expected higher standards from the people whose ancestors made the temples of Khajuraho, those great monoliths with sexual extravaganzas writhing up their stony sides. The Indians sat spellbound by the milkman's limited repertoire, and nobody scoffed even when he rearranged his hostess for another ordinary coupling followed by some run-of-the-mill fellatio. Just at the moment I thought the milkman had finally come up with an original notion, there occurred the customary event in that part of the world: a total power cut. The screen flickered, shivered, and gave up its ghost. Milkman and housewife were destined to be locked in their embrace for some little time, wherever it is fornicators go under such circumstances.

The whole room exhaled slowly and sat for a moment in silence. A servant opened the curtains and raised the windows. The air conditioning had stopped, and already droplets of sweat were running off the noses of the men.

"Tell me the truth," I said to the man next to me, "does that sort of film really get you going?"

"Get me going? I'm so sorry. I don't understand . . ."

"I mean, well, does it excite you?"

"Ahahaha! I see. 'Get me going.' Yes, yes, I see."

He took a handkerchief out of his pocket and mopped his brow.

"Sometimes, and sometimes not," he said. "It is depending. This I will say: it is always consoling to know that one has been doing it properly."

I never learned what was expected of me in Iran, and a few days after the film show the photographer and I returned to London. What I did learn, however, was that men have recourse to pornography for consolation, relief, out of curiosity, or as a means of celebrating their physical selves with more lusty exuberance than their girlfriends or wives or mothers think is nice. The pornographic heroine is all-cunt, the male is all-cock, and there is no fear of being mistaken, of failing, or being cast down by emotional fusses. Her coy objections are never more than an invitation, which, of course, objections can be in real life. A roué I know tells me he reckons seven out of ten women say "don't, don't, don't!" at critical moments in bed, thus forcing any male who takes them seriously either to go ahead in spite of their commands, or desist and settle for a cup of tea. In porn, the female does not put her partners into such a quandary, and more often says "do, do, do!" at least by the time they are actually doing it. In fact, porn insists upon the female's lubricious pleasure and depends upon it; nothing takes place without her enthusiastic participation.

I've watched hard-porn videos with male friends who were not in the least aroused by them because I wasn't. And I wasn't because I did not intend to be. Never had I felt more in control of a sexual experience, and never had I realized so clearly my own latent power and cruelty, or recognized the depth of a man's fearful inhibitions in the presence of a self-contained woman. Even sadomasochism, at all except its outer limit, takes place in porn like a ritual between two consenting adults with a greater complicity between them than exists in many marriages, and with an agreement that is the antithesis of rape.

On the other hand, males born of the female's fantasies

as portrayed in her romantic literature are dominating, aggressive, overbearing, muscular, and infinitely more forceful than the poor bloke in porn, who only wants to get his way with a willing girl. The excitement of the female's fantasy is generated by her struggle, her "don't, don't, don't!", against giving in to a handsome beast. It is a contest she must lose. How else can she win it? A husband is the prize she gets for losing. (It used to be called the booby prize.) Although her early resistance only increases his triumph, she is redeemed from shame by a wedding. Two hundred million romantic novels were sold by Harlequin last year, and every last one of them ended in the promise of a permanent union, happily ever after. So does *Much Ado About Nothing*, and most of the favorite fairy tales of childhood.

"I'm not harboring any grudges against him," says a spirited beauty called Sheri in Harlequin's *Time to Forget*. "I simply find his particular brand of assured superiority utterly insufferable, if you must know!" "He," interchangeable with countless heroes like him, is a broad-shouldered youth, though older of course than Sheri, with "incredibly blue, thickly lashed eyes" that hold a "lazily taunting light" to match his "firmly shaped but sensuous mouth" and his "strong-boned chin with just a hint of a cleft in its purposeful center." He and she play all sorts of titillating push-pull games, until she is utterly, but utterly, overcome. This is rape in slow motion.

" 'Don't worry, princess . . . ' he reassured her in throaty tones. 'I love you, I want you, I need you . . . and not only that, I also intend to marry you as soon as humanly possible . . . so don't say you haven't been warned!' His gleaming white teeth showed in a fascinating smile."

Sheri and her vast army of clones remind me of an earnest, highly educated feminist I heard tell an audience of university girls they ought to "insult three men every day." Insults are an immature form of sexual foreplay, the kind of thing boys and girls do openly at every park and pool. Insults provoke the male to show muscle; they do not lead to discussion, or debate, or revelation. On the contrary, insults lead to a showdown, which the biggest prick must win. There is a new trend in porn for a tough feminist like this one to find herself coerced into making love with a male she has professed to despise. Her defeat by him is not the end of the story, as it was for Sheri; on the contrary, she is overwhelmed, overjoyed, and liberated by the surprising power of her own sexual response. I certainly heard a virginal dare to the male to conquer, penetrate, and satisfy in the feminist's advice.

"Talk nicely to three men every day" would have been a more interesting recommendation, "and find out what makes the bastards tick." This, however, requires an attempt at equality, and males do not often or easily fuck their equals.

Intercourse is an aggressive act, requiring physical strength and even a degree of hostility. Physical penetration would be a painful abasement for a heterosexual man, even if he happened to be attracted to it for reasons of his own. He doesn't offer such indignity to a friend, or put a friend in place with head down, ass up, tongue first, legs apart, all positions the male considers at the very least undignified when he considers them coolly. Some degree of audacity is necessary to any male who wants to get it up, and the closer a female comes to equality, the more difficult it is for him to put her in the postures of his sexual fantasies. The female to some extent probably has to remain an alien of strange, even repellent appetites, so she can be turned into all-cunt. Otherwise, she may reverse the procedure to which mankind owes its continuing existence, and subject him to dehumanizing humiliation. Not all women want this arrangement to change, or find it offensive. One of my platonic friends is a male in his thirties who participates in the relatively playful sadomasochism in vogue currently. My friend swears he is a feminist and he finds women the equal in every way of men; nevertheless, he is bemused to discover that whenever he spanks a girl, she never fails to love him. He has noticed, he tells me, that the feminine passion also blossoms in restraint, at least in handcuffs or silk threads.

"I can understand that," I told him once when he was showing me his *batterie de boudoir*. "Why not?"

"Jesus Christ!" he cried, mistaking my detachment for a more personal curiosity, "I don't want *you* like *that!*"

The more a woman is admired by a man for her achievements, the less easy it is for him to desire her physically, or to have her at all, without fantasizing about someone else. Thus, there is some justice in the accusation that the New Woman is a source of male impotence, a castrator, a cause for divorce and the end of love. An intelligent woman is a catalyst for a man's castration, even though he does it to himself. Infinitely more men have been castrated by other men or have castrated themselves, albeit sometimes the better to serve a goddess or muse, than were ever gelded by a woman's hand. (When a woman castrates a man, it is not her hand she puts to the job.) No man is able to find a female sexy when she is meeting him on his own turf as an active equal. He can't help it. Nor can he help it that in the crunch he is unable to pretend to sexual arousal as effectively as a woman can. The moment a female dares not being loved and steps out into full light is the moment she threatens him with failure.

Let a woman be a male's superior in the worldly sense and she appears to dominate him. Male subservience to female domination holds the rumor of a sexual predilection that is less heroic even than sterile homosexuality. So shaming is the idea of being overcome by a female, a lot of men find themselves unable to perform sexually when a woman takes the lead in lovemaking. (It's my impression that the woman-on-top position advocated during the early days of feminism has given way to doggy-style sex; though this is not openly admitted, younger women friends who are active in the field tell me they have certainly noticed it.) Certain sexual acts suggest the demeaning perversion of male masochism. Nature has assigned the sexes their roles so strictly, there is as yet no way a man can be unmanned without becoming effeminate, or a female can have balls without becoming mannish.

Sex is not love for a man. In his fantasies he designs a sexual accomplice, not a permanent lover. Over and over again the fiction in men's soft-porn magazines embroiders the male romantic ideal: an erotic encounter with a gorgeous wanton who goes off into the sunset alone without leaving so much as a glass slipper under the bed.

"One more bath in the high, small tub, fitting together so cosily," Herbert Goldberg writes in a story called "Annique" from *Penthouse* magazine, "then she was fresh in her linen skirt."

Annique is a French casual lay, so when she says "adieu" after her bath, she knows what she's talking about.

"No one had ever said that to him before. . . . It seemed to mean good-bye forever."

The hero is quite relieved about that final farewell.

"After a few months, something like this was what he had left of her: a memory of Annique in Paris laughing . . . about the foolishness of those who worry about love. . . ."

"Those who worry about love" comprise practically all of womankind. The male delight in lust and impermanence is romantic in its way, until it is matched with the "happily ever after" of women, when it creates a real social problem. Not many females understand what a man thinks he's up to, wallowing in a bath with a French drab when he could be having a deeply meaningful relationship. Even an author as hardheaded as Nancy Friday entitled a book dealing exclusively with male sexual performance and fantasies *Men in Love* rather than *Men in Lust* or *Men Fucking*. Her collection of female sexual fantasies, by the way, is called *My Secret Garden*. I wager that little plot continues to be planted with root vegetables to be laid down for the cosy winters of happily ever after.

When I first arrived in London, I learned a few things about the male's fantasy females. It was at the time when pubic hair was just coming into fashion in men's magazines and big breasts were already becoming a minority taste. This was at the start of the rule of miniskirt and male eyes were lowered for a flash of panties, a trend that led in due course straight to soft porn's focus on the few female inches to remain hidden in polite society. I had been living in Paris (a very prudish city, by the way) and I arrived in London with less than the fare back home to America in my pocket, the first condition required for becoming an expatriate. I was broke, out of work, and scared. One evening as I nursed a half of lager in a pub near my one-room apartment, and wondered where it was all going to end, I heard my name called. There stood an Englishman I'd met briefly years earlier in Spain. He seemed pleased to see me again; he offered me a drink, and we talked about the bull-running festival in Pamplona where we had met, a mecca for young heroes who sprint in front of the charging bulls, and flood the streets with braggadocio and sometimes with blood. Little was I to know as I raised my gin and tonic that the friendly acquaintance was going to drag me into the hellholes of Soho and through the Fleet Street gutters.

My degradation began on the spot when he hired me to work for his publicity firm and write press releases for something called "The Revue Bar." The very next night, off I went with clean pad and brand-new pencil to what in my ignorance I assumed was one of the underground satirical review theaters popular in London at that time. Underground, it certainly was. Satirical? In a way. I'll never forget one astonishing act when the stage was flooded and frozen so the strippers, blue with cold, could skate naked figure eights in front of an audience that was oddly docile, all men, sitting straight and separate, hearing only the sound of their own breathing, like spacemen locked into helmets.

Not long afterward, our impresario decided to start the first English girlie magazine, and overnight I found myself no longer a publicist, rather one of an editorial board poring over transparencies of women with no clothes on. Our biggest problem was not in finding women who would strip for the camera, it was in stopping those who shouldn't. Droves of females applied in answer to our advertisement. We saw photographs of naked housewives, naked secretaries, naked bank clerks and schoolgirls, as well as a lot of professional strippers, taut and depilated as marble. After a few weeks, I began to understand what the men preferred in stroke-princesses. While I always chose bones, strong lines, and faces that looked as if they could spit in an eye at twenty paces, my male colleagues went for the dimple, the pout and the pink. When it came to their sexual icons they liked a tootsie who advertised her availability yet managed to persuade each voyeur it was for him alone she was arching her back and sweeping her hair up from the back of her neck. They wanted neither a threat nor a victim, only a quality of cheerful acquiescence I soon learned to recognize, a face and posture that promised wholehearted, unquestioning acceptance of whatever was on offer: the sort of girl a man could love and leave, simply by turning a page. The smallest trace of embarrassment in the girl's smile or in her eyes embarrassed the men, any hint of the film star's self-satisfied narcissism also put them off, and so did the sleek, costly beauty of a fashion model. Whether intelligence would have discouraged them as well, I can only guess; there wasn't much of it in evidence either in the photographs or the letters that accompanied them. Soft porn's nudes look straight out from the pages of stroke-magazines. They know what they're doing there. They aren't Degas girls surprised in a moment of concentration, or great walloping Rubens nudes, too indolent to turn their heads; they are more like eager salesgirls with a "that will do nicely, sir" gleam in their eyes. Although sometimes they drop their lashes under a coy weight, they never laugh, and they almost always have long hair. They're clean and safe except in some hard porn where their threat is a wild promise. Nowadays, when the models open and display their sex, they still look straight into the sucker's eyes, just the way a grocer does when he assures his customer the mango is ripe.

I quit the magazine when I was owed so much back pay I felt justified in helping myself to a book of beautiful Japanese prints that showed robed couples making intense love, their sex organs carefully drawn in a welter of brocades, while mice and chipmunks watched impassively from the edges of the page. Being broke as ever, I tried to peddle the book in Soho porn shops, in itself an instructive experience.

"Lovely book, madame, really lovely," one porn merchant told me. "The trouble is it just isn't dirty enough."

Soft porn magazines invite masturbation. Men masturbate a lot in their lifetimes, and they often do it before the image of a centerfold goddess. Letters from the users of girlie magazines praise the unknown female fingering her genitalia for the camera, and thank her for the acts of solitary rejoicing she allows them.

"I couldn't believe it when I looked at Trudy Pickford in 'Knave.' . . . she is the most extravagantly gorgeous example of the perfect female form. . . ." writes a typical reader. "I wish her every success in her photographic career . . . ."

Porn magazines are mostly a visual medium; they do,

however, need to fill spaces between pictures. When the editors run short of salacious written material, they print interviews with the male and female "stars" of hard-porn videos. In July 1984, for instance, *Hustler* talked to a sex star called Mai Lin about her career, and in the way she discusses her job is a detachment that exemplifies the absence of emotional involvement men want from fantasy fucks. The item reminded me of an interview I myself had years ago in the north of England with a woman called Anne, who worked on an assembly line for bottled pie fillings:

> **Mai Lin:** "Four years ago I did a picture called 'Mai Lin versus Serena.' In the final scene Serena and I have this contest: Whoever fucks the most guys gets the starring role in an adult film."
>
> (**Anne:** "Seniority counts . . . but in the end it's down to how much you work, if you want to become a supervisor. . . .")
>
> **Mai Lin:** "So I'm in this pink bathtub, and about forty guys in masks hop in and start fucking me. . . . That was the hardest movie I'd ever done. . . ."
>
> (**Anne:** "Before my wedding I did so much overtime my mum threw water on me in the morning to wake me up; I was that tired. . . .")
>
> **Mai Lin:** "I was doing anal . . . one time and tore myself. . . . It took three years to fully recuperate. . . ."
>
> (**Anne:** "The worst are blackberries. . . . You can't wash the stains off. . . . They take ages to finally wear off. . . .")

Angry feminists say pornography demeans women by presenting them as sex objects, yet hundreds of women write to advice columns complaining that their boyfriend's pornography makes them feel they aren't sex object enough. It isn't easy for any woman to understand the male's atavistic gusto or his quick, infallible celebration before the image of cunt. As long as women see sex as love they are bound to be miffed when men offer to the open air what they feel should be pledged to them. Males, however, consider jerking off to be an act altogether different from sexual intercourse, and a more basic, urgent rite than most females think sex ought to be. When a woman masturbates, she uses the image of her beloved, or she creates an imaginary hero who stars in a complicated scenario. Women are inventive and fanciful masturbators, weaving climaxes out of memories and secrets, while the male is content with a paper image. Whether a woman considers porn and pinups demeaning to her sex depends upon whether she considers that male sexuality has a more brutish function than her own, which, once upon a time, engendered the future, though now it is more often sterile and love-mad.

The page 3 cutie pinned on the locker-room door inspires the same sort of automatic reverence as religious medals on the dashboards of Greek taxi drivers. Men on subway trains in the morning don't fidget in unbearable sexual excitement over the tits of the tabloids laid out before them, though maybe for a while their boredom is lessened a little. Any male free from trauma or inhibition enjoys the sight of an attractive female body, whether it is the one he is pledged to love and honor or not. When he is despondent, it cheers him, when he is fretful, it soothes him; and when he is in danger it reminds him bodies were not given us merely so that we could dispatch them to kingdom come. Soldiers in World War II didn't care any less for their sweethearts because Betty Grable was the hero's pinup. With Grable on the wall, a sweetheart in his wallet, and Mum safe at home, any soldier was in possession of powerful "talis-women" and distaff magic. The girl on page 3 is an object, that's true, and yet no more so than the bank manager's wife framed in silver on his desk. One object represents heroism, infallibility and sexual vigor; the other, comfort, security, affection and habit.

A male friend of mine calls his susceptibility to visual images the "flash mechanism," and he says it is as ancient in malekind as the heartbeat of the hunter when the prey comes into sight. In his experience, which happens to be vast, men respond sexually to pictures, and women to the more wistful, intimate allure of the word. Males turn images into action, and women turn their fantasies into motives for love. The instantaneous response to what he sees is part of a young man's sexuality, intrinsic to it, even necessary to it. To shame him for this quirk could cause us all considerable harm, because his sexuality is dependent upon his ego. It is as much due to the male's ego as to his sperm that humankind keeps on reproducing. Nevertheless, these days, both male ego and male sperm are being routinely frozen. The ability men have to lust joyfully at the sight of the female, and then to fuck without commitment, is being seen increasingly as contemptible. There are people who consider it acceptable for him to impregnate, mechanically or physically, a surrogate mother so that his barren mate can fulfill her need to raise a child, yet at the same time consider him less than an animal if he jerks off, is unfaithful, or pays a whore to fulfill his need for infallibility.

The female worries about love a lot. The male, for reasons of his spirit as well as his triggerish flesh—even in spite of his best intentions—worries about losing the archaic thrust, and longs sometimes not to give a fuck, only to take one. It demands greater generosity and more control than women realize, or need to show in their own lives, for a man not to dream he is a conqueror among the females, or at least to want to dream that way. All our taboos and laws dealing with sex, especially the laws of marriage, require the male to control his penis and watch out where he puts it. Most men are law-abiding and willing to please up to the threshold of failure, even past it. However, current demands make it almost impossible for a man to do the right thing sexually

without sacrificing freedom, independence, robust maleness, pleasure and hilarity, to the female's cry for fidelity,
eternal love, security, and, more recently, equality from acts
perpetrated by the human penis. It also confuses any
thoughtful man that women advertise loudly for mates who
are considerate, gentle, full of foreplay and respect, and then
they fantasize and fall for men who are bold, overbearing,
"firmly-shaped," self-assured, wicked, and real fuckers.

I used to know a man who was well-bred, worn and
dusty, like a piece of furniture in a grand household that
can no longer afford to keep servants. Among his drinking
companions was a loudmouth of the type who attracts
masochists and then fails to deliver what they bargained for.
My suave acquaintance told me once how thrilled he had
been when this overweight boor reached forward as they
were walking in the street, and lifted his wife's skirt from
behind, presumably to show off what a fine piece of goods
he possessed, and how she didn't wear panties. My friend's
eye glittered when he told this story, and he tapped his foot
nervously, in the way a girlfriend and I, comparing notes
in our teens, noticed men do when sexual arousal is just
beginning to twitch. This expensively educated chap of some
social rank lusted after a woman who would let him make
a pig of himself, instead of the lightweight with lovely manners his mother had raised. He adored and resented the
haughty goddesses of his own caste with whom he dared
not take gross liberties; he desired a woman he would not
be required to respect, a slave who would let him be captor
and boss. (He thought being in charge and being free were
compatible conditions. It is a mistake men often make.)

It so happens, my dusty friend had been divorced by his
wife of thirty years in bitterness over a frivolous love affair.
His life had been a shambles and his integrity destroyed by
the grinding of desire against propriety. One hundred years
ago, or even the day before yesterday, he could have stayed

married to the respectable mother of his children, and done rude things to "bad" girls. Now, such sexual expediency leads to divorce courts or to counselors who "cure" men of the unfashionable desire to make free from time to time with a willing female. It can be so fraught, so threatening, for a male to have the bold, invigorating, straightforward sexual union of his fantasy even inside marriage that it is surprising so many men keep on trying. It is not surprising many of them aren't convinced they want to try, or that some prefer to pay for a sure thing. It is even less surprising that vast numbers are deciding it is not natural or necessary for them to make love to females whose cervixes are hermetically or chemically sealed, and who demand a mystical kick and commitment out of their sexual encounters. Men are being strapped into romantic monogamy; it is a process some of them find as crippling as the binding of feet was for Chinese females, and to the man who dares question it, just as perverse. Maybe some day the female's dream of intercourse as a rapturous, exclusive, eternal expression of true love, separate from lust or procreation, will bring the sexes into glorious unity; for the moment, however, her passionate extortion is increasing the market for hard porn and divorce lawyers, as men are finding it ever more difficult to squeeze themselves and their erections into the shrinking maneuvering space between being a wimp or being a rapist.

3
MARRIAGE

There is one hurdle few men survive with spirit intact, one journey that fuddles their instincts, one contract they find it hard to fulfill with honor, and one battle that leaves them bleeding on the field or scampering for shelter. It is the triumph of Cinderella over *Hustler* and Homer, the overtaking of imagination by common sense, and the defeat of caprice by etiquette; it is marriage or, to use the modern euphemism appropriate to the coaxing of men into an institution, it is his "commitment." Unless a man weds Penelope, who is happy to tat at home while he carouses with the lads and fools around with Circe, he must commit to the past all his playful dreams and adventures at the very altar that is the end and aim of hers. Wedding bells summon a man back to the nursery from the playground this whole planet used to be for him, and the marriage license is seen by his bride as a permit to begin his reformation and transformation into husband.

Despite the orange blossom and yards of tulle, weddings are commonplace events. Marriage is not much more than a tidy box in which two compatible people can raise a family. Until recently, matrimony seemed to be the only practical solution to the perplexities of the female's social condition; ideally it gave her a purpose, status, babies and shelter, while giving her husband comfort, heirs, authority, and a considerable amount of freedom. Marriage kept money, title and property moving around, or united them as it still does in aid of dynasty. Not long ago, a couple would have been ashamed to declare publicly they were marrying because they were in love rather than for security, family, and the affection that can grow out of sharing a serious undertaking. The modern Western couple, however, especially if they are marrying for money or status, advertise their love. Love is all this fabulous commitment requires. There are even clergymen in our society ready to marry homosexual couples because they are in love, and want a certificate to prove it.

No doubt monogamous marriage has always caused men and women a degree of misery. Romantic monogamy that encourages both sexes to marry for love, and only love, is, however, a slow killer with a feminine bias. Everyone supposed young women had been liberated to become brain surgeons, and independent masters of their own destinies; yet, they will choose instead to race pell-mell into torrid romantic novels where their vaunted feelings take precedence over experience and knowledge. Brides-to-be actually think they are going to live "happily ever after," and love must prevail over any who would gainsay it, even a spouse already in residence. Binding contracts are being made every day without any detached counsel, based on an emotion that is by definition ephemeral, and signed by two people who are not in their right minds. (In-love is unquestionably a form of temporary insanity corresponding roughly to the in-heat frenzy of other animals.) No intelligent person would set up a corner shop in such a manner, let alone a household and a new line in human beings.

To my surprise I noticed early on that for every marriage there is a man. (For every divorce there is one too.) Soon I learned to distinguish married men from free young heroes by a quality in their commerce with available females that is at the same time furtive and smug. I have always been dismayed by how many husbands there are. I know if I were a man I wouldn't pledge myself to one woman until I was damn sure all fires had been banked. The "lock" in wedlock would put me off. Nor would I dream of making marriage the center of my life; on the contrary, it could only be a sideline. Commitment is a great, mysterious achievement involving faith and surrender. When fortunate women have it with their babies it's called "maternal bonding." Commitment has always been what heroes search for in life: a god revealed in one moment of truth, a truth revealed in one moment of understanding, not only a reason for joy and pain, but also their purpose. No human being can or should be all this for another.

Even when I was a little girl, family funerals were more to my taste than weddings. The emotion at funerals was genuine and moving, the prayers were elegant, the commitment was certainly ineluctable, and nobody wagged a finger at me by the graveside, saying: "You'll be next!" (It's fair to add that I have received only one real proposal in my life. It was from a bent poet who wrote blank verse and lived on cornflakes with mayonnaise that he stole from the local supermarket. He laughed when I turned him down, then went on to marry a few of my friends in sequence and in due course to write a Broadway hit.) I wasn't far into my twenties before I noticed that the only unmarried men left were homosexuals, a few tireless playboys, and some writers. It struck me that among artists, the group of men I have always found attractive, heterosexual painters were already married, probably to save model fees. Because they like to move in schools, they also tended to exchange their wives monotonously. Actors attached themselves to anyone who polished their mirrors. Only writers seemed sometimes to stay single, no doubt in order to preserve and protect the ego from which they, in solitude, draw everything.

Most young men fall in love where it flatters them and then marry out of other weaknesses. A man marries because he's afraid if he doesn't, she'll cry (guilt). Because he doesn't want people to think he's a homosexual (bigotry). Because he is a homosexual (hypocrisy). Because he lacks stamina to keep his own house (laziness). Because she makes him feel sexy and she says it's love (lust and gullibility). Because she's pregnant (despair). Because he wants heirs (hubris). Because he's afraid to be alone (cowardice). Because it's high time he showed everyone how grown up he is (immaturity). Because he's tired of playing games (futility). Because she wants it and he can always play around on the side (cynicism). Because it's only a piece of paper, and what difference can it make? (naïveté). There are also some men so unsure of their sexual and intellectual powers they dream of uncritical conquest such as a milkmaid, say, or a slave, or a virgin, or the woman of a defeated class; and it can happen that such a man mates with a female from a race he actually despises. Miscegenation can be an expression of racism. By the same token, there are men who marry in order to protect themselves against the predatory host of women, and these unions can be seen as an expression of what is currently called "sexism."

A man has his reasons to marry, good or bad. A woman, however, is probably marrying out of an impossible romance. She expects security and fidelity, loving sex, constant attention, flowing communication, heaps of sensitized emoting, a house, adorable babies, a decent car and, having been liberated, she expects equality too, as if it were his to give. Altogether, she requires everything unliberated womankind ever did from marriage, and a lot more. What she brings to the match, however, is considerably less than women have in the past. Sometimes, she'll cook on alternate nights and wash half the dishes; often she will earn less than her husband though she'll spend as much; and as for children, she'll have some someday, only not yet. There are even brides who say they don't intend to have babies at all, not ever, which makes their marriage licenses about as appropriate as gun permits for water pistols. The fact is, a manless woman in our society still sees herself as a botched pot on the shelf, and is still seen that way by many other people, while a heterosexual bachelor of normal appearance and appetites is widely admired by his own sex and will not lack for the company of women when he wants it.

Everyone agrees piously that sex is not the most important aspect of marriage; however, in truth, marital intercourse has to run a pretty close second to a joint bank account, certainly for a young couple who have no children. Sexual intercourse is probably one of the first things a couple do together after their wedding. It is the only thing they are expected to continue doing together, and in theory it is the only thing either of them is prohibited from ever doing again with anyone else. The marriage certificate is a license to screw blamelessly, honestly, interminably. Indeed, the man had better avail himself of that right or the whole business can be annulled. These days there isn't much chance either partner is a virgin and less that they both are, so even though ghastly Victorian honeymoon blunders are unlikely, the price paid is that neither of them is going to imagine that when they achieve sexual pleasure it is a piece of magic peculiar to their union. Probably the pair have already made love and maybe they have been living together; nevertheless, postmarital sex begins in a flutter of excitement. Not only is it entitled to luxurious privacy, but it radiates an exhibitionist *frisson* among in-laws, tradesmen, friends, enemies, desk clerks and chambermaids, who know married people make love and assume newlyweds do it a lot. Dirty jokes are told by men after weddings because of the bride's sexy freshness, and mascara runs during the ceremony because women are already seeing the phantom pram in her wake. Newlyweds encourage onlookers to think about sex, and that encourages newlyweds to be sexy. There are cohabiting couples who decide to marry at last because their love-making needs a fillip. Often, the bride is titillated by the complete rightness and rectitude of her new status, while her groom, servant and husband, is made feverish by the pleasures now and forever at his bidding. Or he is desperately trying to assuage in an orgy of lust the suspicion that he has just made the most dreadful mistake. A lot of men have told me they realized before their weddings that they loved freedom more than their brides and were on the brink of disaster. It was just that things had gone too far, and suicidal chivalry prevailed. When I've had similar confidences from women, their hesitation was always because another suitor was hanging around in the shadows. It wasn't the choice between marriage and freedom that bothered them so much as a feeling they loved the other more than the man in hand.

Even though any man can be lured into a web with some beads and a few mirrors, human males are mating creatures, not essentially marrying ones, and they become restless in time. They start to struggle against the strands that enfolded them once so sweetly and now threaten to strangle them. Whenever what was free choice becomes a duty, irksome responsibilities are the result. Give a man permission and license to fish but one mile of a river that once was all his, and the nature of his sport changes. Even though he still enjoys the fishing, his delight has become enclosed by moral and legal fences. Let him stray just once, or even look as though he'd like to, to some enticing inlet upstream, and he is not an admirable, adventurous sportsman, just a trespasser, a poacher, and a criminal who is liable to prosecution. If his patch of river has turned out to be sterile, turbulent, or running dry, and there is no more sport left in it for him, he is allowed only to forget, or to remember behind a bland mask, or to re-create alone his old ecstasy when the silver beast, now becoming extinct, leaps gasping into the air. Even if he's fond of his bit of river, its pleasures must become predictable; even if he loves it, love is not the engrossing pursuit for him it is for women, and it is not sex. Eventually, if the struggling ego within him clamors for the old strum and tickle, the male enters what is called mid-life crisis, when he has been known to run off with a minnow from the typing pool.

After the first delirium, marriage becomes a battle between two egos. Generally, his takes a bigger beating, because he had more to begin with. The woman who made him feel a giant is making him feel a mouse who has taken the cheese. Sex is a barometer of love for her; as far as he is concerned, however, his penis is the puppet of his ego, and in marriage it often begins to wilt as his beaming bride starts to show sexual impatience or indifference in a way she never did during courtship. Unmarried women invariably write to advice columnists when they are afraid their inability to achieve orgasm (which doesn't bother them personally because love is more important) will make their lovers feel inadequate, and drive them elsewhere for a more flattering fuck. Married women with the same problem write in a pique that their husbands are not skilled enough to make them "come." (These are nonorgasmic females, of course. I made the mistake of using the word "frigid" in a column recently and received a bagful of hate letters for daring to suggest any woman had a sexual dysfunction that wasn't her partner's fault.)

A man's bride will one day begin to tell her husband that he hasn't any feelings and is not capable of understanding what she feels. It's not easy for him, hating scenes as he does, to get through to a woman who is in the throes of being sensitive, or to tell her truthfully that he does have feelings; he is feeling trapped, impotent, restless and scared. Her swift, angry reactions censor anything he says that she cannot bear to hear. From this point on, he will probably begin to withdraw, possibly shouting those classic words of Mantalk to a frenzied woman: "You're crazy!" which actually means she's driving him mad.

Sometimes, of course, she really is crazy, perhaps driven mad by him. It happens that to drive a wife stark, staring mad is a theme in melodrama borrowed from life. One way for a husband to rescue his ego from his wife's grip, is to deprive her of self-control. If she can't control herself, she can't control him. Once a man has driven his wife around the bend, he can be self-indulgent, egotistical, and unfaithful, with impunity denied other men; he will even be forgiven social and professional failure because, only look at what the sainted soul has to put up with at home. Some husbands discover ways to make their wives make them suffer excruciatingly, exquisitely, as nobody ever made them suffer before. A provocative husband is able to rouse his wife's fury quite deliberately not because he loves suffering, rather because he hankers for marital sainthood, and for the reverence of all who behold it. I've seen many men who can only trust themselves to be "good" husbands to women who are patently, screamingly "bad." One of these marital martyrs told me with a brave smile how his wife had flown at him like an angry hornet while he was at the wheel of their speeding car.

"Gosh!" I said, "what must you have done to provoke her!"

"Nothing," he replied, with bowed head. "Absolutely nothing."

People who fly into murderous, suicidal rages on highways for no reason at all are put away sooner or later for long periods of time. This wife, I suspect, went mad only when her husband pushed a few secret buttons guaranteed to send her into overdrive. In front of their friends and family, he'd set her off, then be deeply solicitous, so that he became an admired, saintly fellow who was excused his affairs, his incipient alcoholism, and his frequent silliness. They were only to be expected, poor chap.

In the great long ago, a husband could pacify the sickly hero of his soul and his own disappointed youth with an occasional fun-loving, forgettable girl on the side. Now, though there is no shortage of girls who want to play, a married man is not strictly taboo for serious expectations. All a female has to do is persuade herself she is really, really in love to excuse any dalliance to her conscience, even ennoble it. It's not at all unusual for an advice column to receive letters from women in love with married men "forever" and unable to live without them, who see the legal mate and children as stubborn obstructions to a joy that was meant to be. And does he not swear he hasn't touched his spouse since two years before the birth of their last child? No married man will have trouble finding extramarital sex these days, though he may have a hard time avoiding it, and he's bound to have a devilish time getting rid of it. It's not only wives who have become more demanding of men, mistresses have too, and to service more than one woman for whom sex is love can be crippling.

"I wish I were homosexual!" was the despairing cry of the only married man whose other woman I was for a time.

"We met on a plane," said the husband in a recent television drama when he was caught out in adultery, "we had a couple of drinks . . . she started flirting with me . . . and . . . well . . . I didn't mean it to happen . . ." Somebody must mean it to happen. Presumably, she did. Insecurity, boredom, fatigue, fear and distraction can all prevent any man from an erection; apparently fidelity cannot do as much. To some degree, the man must mean it to happen, or it can't. Very few husbands end their days under a halo of absolute fidelity, and experienced wives ask only that they should not be told, or embarrassed before their friends. As any woman who has been the mistress of a married man knows, the wife holds stronger cards: children, habit, and a massive claim on his income. Infidelity by a wife, however, continues to be a different matter, not simply because of custom and the rights of possession, but because where she fucks she falls in love, while he just loves fucking. Moreover, she is the one who can do children harm by bringing their paternity into question. Be a woman be-coiled or on the pill, the fact is sex has a function and a potential for her that it cannot have for a man. Even when contraception becomes infallible (and not susceptible to human error) it is doubtful that wifely fidelity will ever be merely a matter of courtesy, as it is for husbands.

I myself have never met a persistently unfaithful husband who was noticeably happy. The fact that fidelity is difficult does not make it any the less part of the marriage deal, and husbands who can't stick it are in a worrying condition of bad faith. Infidelity isn't called "cheating" for nothing. Furthermore, when a wife discovers her husband is straying, she either makes their home life hell or she takes vengeance-lovers and turns the union into a sham. Precisely because females now are generally demanding of males, a wife knows full well her husband is giving more than a fuck to her rival: he's giving time, he's giving expensive dinners, he's giving intimacy, he's giving conversation, he's giving hope, and he's giving at least a semblance of emotional involvement. Sexual jealousy is not irrational. Even the celebrated "open marriages" of the 1960s were soon infected with it, their futile agreements undermined by the inequities nature has put upon the sexes. Usually, the husbands were more enthusiastically unfaithful than their mates; though I know one couple where it was the wife who cut a swath through the forest of delight until the day—the very moment, even

—he found a bright, pretty girl eager to help him restore his ego (by that time it was about the size of a mosquito bite); whereupon did that "open marriage" ever slam closed with a bang!

Here and there are to be found sinning husbands who replace the thrill of premarital sex with the tension of marital deception. They like to see what pitch of guilt they can achieve before they spill the beans. It's an endurance test that keeps a man in a state of high excitement, sometimes two or three times a night, until the going is too easy and boredom threatens; then he does something dangerous: leaves a hotel bill in his pocket, carries the wrong brand of cigarettes, or smells of something sweeter than aftershave. In the aftermath of the resultant cataclysm, marital sex is restored to its old delight and the other woman is discarded until the next time.

Marriage shares with other institutions the power to institutionalize its inmates. If it didn't, the divorce rate would be even higher than it is. Divorce has less to do with extramarital lechery than with lack of patience. People in love are in a frenetic dither, and when the searing, blinding flame flickers, then subsides, they are left with nothing, only ashes and an impatient longing to chuck the whole mess and try again. There is a general pattern to most marriages: long honeymoon, followed by short turbulence, another long honeymoon, more turbulence, shorter honeymoons, longer turbulence, babies, upheaval, disappointment, possible infidelities, turbulence, and then at last if it is ever to arrive, the calm of two chastened wills, not ecstatically happy perhaps, certainly happier than they could ever be apart. It seems a shame that marriage can't be saved as a retirement plan for sensible grown-ups after the children have left home.

The frequency of modern divorce is creating new patterns for men and women, which deserve attention because solutions to marital problems may be found among them. A husband who divorces between infidelities and eventual serenity has already been half reformed and he will marry again as soon as he can, to have the process resolved. Sometimes, he and his first wife will hate the sight of each other; just as often, however, he will remember her fondly while he repeats the frantic stages of settling into his second marriage. He'll probably see his first wife regularly too, and doubtless go to bed with her from time to time. As a rule second wives tend to be more jealous of their predecessors than first wives of their successors, and they have reason to be: number one wife keeps a share of her ex-husband's time and almost always holds a chunk of his money. A remarried divorced man can learn that as far as his bank manager is concerned, he has two wives. Surely, it's only a matter of time before the to-ing and fro-ing of males in the mate market, where females are more numerous, will begin to provide imaginative remedies to the loneliness, frustration and desperation of married, aging women.

I lived with a clever, prosperous man for about two years. It was an amicable experiment that neither altogether failed nor really succeeded, and we parted in good humor. Three years or so later, he rang to tell me he was about to be married. Eight years later, he was divorced and remarried. He and I still enjoyed each other and I saw him from time to time when his new wife, a model, was abroad; occasionally without fuss or wild excitement, he stayed the night. I knew he was seeing his first wife, too, in the house he had bought for her and their daughters.

"What a louse! Aren't men the pits?" a romantic young friend said when I told her about this loose harem.

Personally, I didn't agree. I enjoy the company of an attentive, attractive man once in a while. However, I can't work worth a fig when I'm in love, so the arrangement suited me very well. His first wife didn't object either. "The only trouble with that marriage," the man told me once, "was that she mothered me all the time. Sex with her feels like a kind of cure. Something to make it better. Sometimes that's just what the doctor ordered, you might say, but it starts to be awfully predictable. I do love her in a way, and," he added, "she's great with the kids." This, it so happens, is Mantalk for "she prefers the kids to me."

One night, I went alone to a concert and during the interval I saw my tall friend's head rising above the crowd. I waved to him, he waved back. I thought he looked a little flushed. The crowds parted, and at his side I saw his second wife, a stunning girl in a dress that made her pregnancy look like a voguish accessory.

"She's the most beautiful thing I've ever seen," he had said of her. "Mind you, when she grapples with an idea, it's like a kitten with a ball of wool." It was too late to retreat, so we all three made highly animated small talk, and his second wife asked if I would join them for dinner after the concert. To be honest, I think I would probably have refused, were it not that just as the bell was ringing we heard a joyous shout, and there was wife number one; plump, bustling, wearing shades of potato and aubergine. She had come to the concert with friends who were driving back to the country afterward and, yes, she was free and why didn't we make a party for dinner?

At the restaurant, the male was distinctly nervous, while we three women got on famously. His first wife told his second wife how to make yogurt, and his second wife gave me the name of her hairdresser.

"Another whiskey, please. A large one," said our mutual man to the waiter.

"He will . . ." said the first wife.

". . . do that," said the second.

"One of these days," I said, "his liver will be sent back to the kitchen."

He filled his first wife's glass with wine, lit my cigarette, passed the bread rolls to his second wife.

"Thank you," said the first wife.

"Darling," said the second.

I winked at him and blew smoke in his eyes, the way he'd always hated me to.

Looking round our happy party, I thought what a weird and irresistible trio we three women made. It takes three women to outnumber one man. Two women can be played off against each other so that one of them sides with the male in mockery, but three women in concert must tease, control and triumph over any man, as they surround him in the classic postures of wife, mother, mistress. Put a male among three females who like each other, I thought, watching our man sample the food on his first wife's plate (he always did that) and he'll be lucky indeed to escape before he's turned into a serious, adult member of society. Or even a frog.

4

FATHERHOOD

S ooner or later, most men want to start a family, and a little bit sooner women want to have babies. Fortuitous coincidence though this is, it is not the same thing. A father-to-be can change his mind about a family, while his pregnant mate is bound to have a baby. The urge to make a family is dynastic and cerebral; it can be indulged without physiological change, without discomfort, and without passion. Childbirth, on the other hand, entails major physiological changes, some of them mysterious; and unexpected passions, some of them dark. Parturition is one of the three natural experiences in life from which, once it is under way, no effort of will or body can remove the subject, who is also the object; it is furthermore the only primary animal experience exclusive to the female. Simply being able to participate in it, even choosing not to, determines femaleness. Giving birth demands a donation of the pregnant woman's body and a commitment of her ego beyond any customarily required of a man. It's a great reminder of mortality. Meanwhile, father hands out cigars and buys extra life insurance because he has proudly set in motion his own particle of immortality. A baby is made because of her instinct and his urge; these are two vastly different forces.

Between fathering and mothering lie all the differences between the sexes: decision and feeling, action and reaction, propulsion and gestation, and love, which is sometimes the greatest difference of all. The female's recent selection of sex as her metaphor for love can be seen as an attempt to honor the phenomenon of birth with which she is infinitely more involved than the male; or it can be seen as a way to dignify female contraception, only recently as widely available to nice girls as it has always been, one way or another, to whores. There can be no doubt the single most important sexual event to happen to men in past decades happened to women; the female's acquisition of contraceptive methods almost as infallible as chastity is as close as human beings have come to controlling nature, and even to excluding her from a natural function. What is the sex act so far as nature is concerned save a pragmatic bang with no purpose except to deliver seed to the sole fertile place where it can begin the haphazard miracle of new life? People of both sexes swear they felt the sperm hit its target and knew the very moment conception began. Why disbelieve them? When such a momentous conjoining takes place, it seems logical that the human beings involved may understand what they have done. An eminent member of the Asian community in Bristol told me that the partners in arranged marriages learn to love each other after this shared experience; among us others, however, love is supposed to come first, so excusing and justifying our sterile encounters. If fucking for fun instead of love, or at least posterity, ever finally becomes the sole aim and purpose of female maturity, then the source of decadence will be women. Women now put themselves in charge of love and emotions where once they were in charge of the nursery; if they don't, they will lose altogether any claim to their traditional role as a moral restraint on society. This is a position females have held not because of any innate goodness but simply because they carried the next generation, and were ambassadors for the innocent future. The demands on men now to participate in birth, which is literally none of their business, are being made in the name of love and also in an attempt to clarify the role of father so that men are as snug in it as women have always been in the role of mother.

Paternity is open to question in a way maternity cannot be. I've met plenty of men who think perhaps they fathered a child somewhere. Has anyone ever met a sane woman who didn't know for sure when she had given birth? The act of intercourse for a female can last nine months, and if there were no manufactured contraceptives or gallant vasectomies, she could be pregnant or lactating for twenty years or more of her adult life. Whether a female undertakes it or not, she is born to a profession that is closed to males. When a couple want offspring that the wife cannot produce, the agony of sterility is greater for her, and her sexual humiliation is comparable to that of an impotent male. Each baby who existed in her heart, for whom her body was unable to provide transport, requires mourning in all its stages of denial, anger, agony, grief and finally, acceptance. There is often great affection within barren marriages, and a childless husband who stays the course can become an unusually gentle, docile mate out of shared disappointment and sympathy for his wife's suffering. Furthermore, because the union is spared the upheaval even the most beloved intruder imposes, he is not deprived of his spouse's attention; on the contrary he receives more of it than ever, and enough to enslave him. If a woman has children, she pays a price; and if she does not have them, she pays a price. Women *will* mother: cats, a cause, aspidistras, men, or at the very worst, themselves. Among my circle of close friends are a number of women, now middle-aged, who have chosen to remain childless; and in all except one of these personalities is sharp bitterness, and a tendency to intellectual or physical self-indulgence. A woman barren by election can swell to fill her own nursery. At best she devotes herself to good works for which she may even win the honorary title of "mother," or "matron," or "dame." Childless men do not run the same risk of regret and disappointment because the ability to carry the next generation is not built into them, they have no physiological drive to paternity, and their participation in childbirth is a matter of choice.

Even now that parturition is not always, or often, desirable, sex can work for a female in an awesome way of which she is aware from the day she buys her first box of Tampax. When she is pregnant, her mate practices breathing with her, watches the ripples on her bath water, makes love to her in medically acceptable positions, even adores her; maybe he sees the crown of his baby's head hit the air for the first time and hears its first cry. Nevertheless, there is a moment when she is seized by the convulsion of birth and part of her is claimed by a vocation he cannot share and from which he is excluded.

"Good girl!" everyone says to her, then. "Well done!"

For her man, possessed by fear of failure, her commitment and triumph can bring a troubling doubt about his ability to play second fiddle with good grace.

When my son was born, I spent two months prior to delivery in what hospitals call "a waiting ward" where I lay in with other women having problematical pregnancies. (In my case, the problem turned out not to be much more than my great age for a first delivery.) It happened to be "Ward 2B," so I used to call it "2B or not 2B." I hadn't lived in such a large company of females since schooldays and never had I lived with so many nonvirgins. Only at first did I resent my incarceration, for it soon turned into a period of emotional intensity and revelation that neatly divided my life into before and after. To give birth is in a sense to be reborn, to see the world differently, to lose some feelings, and gain others. There was a bond among us women on the ward that men can only mimic in the rigmarole of secret societies; it was beyond family or friendship and it easily tolerated hysteria, lunacy, vanity and delusion. The bond passed soon after our babies were born. When we all met at postnatal clinics, we were no longer in communion, having become once again the complements of our menfolk, wearing clothes that displayed their income and distracted by whatever burdens—nannies, meat and two veg, subsistence budgeting—their ranks put upon us. Nevertheless, the passing of the power we shared cannot diminish its reality. Every evening, during visiting hours, the fathers-to-be marched through the swinging doors and posted themselves at our bedsides where they offered flowers and shy conversation. Once in a while, one of the men ran amok and rushed off to try his indignation and frustration on Matron, leaving us women nodding like a Greek chorus.

"Husband creating again, I see," I said to the girl in the bed opposite mine.

She shifted a little. She'd had three miscarriages in the past, and had been on an intravenous drip off and on for most of the month.

"Well, you know how men are. His mother keeps telling him all her babies popped out like eggs."

As soon as their time was up, the ragged ranks would leave us to settle back into our shared night. A bluish light flickered at the nurses' station and the silence of the room was rarely broken by the coughs, groans and snores a young nurse told me filled the night-watch with jungle sounds in Men's Medical. Sometimes when I look at my tall son now, I remember the deep magic we women made together; and I have an inkling of the fear that is part of any wise man's response to the female.

When a marriage breaks up, the children are still more often given into their mother's care, which, contrary to

Hollywood fiction, usually suits everyone. It isn't because of a flawed moral sense fathers feel no guilt when they go to work in the morning, leaving their offspring behind; it's because they aren't mothers. Working mothers, on the other hand, feel very guilty when they have to leave babies who were recently their intimate lodgers and whose whimpers can still make their breasts run like fountains. Guilt may be a rotten feeling, but that does not make it unreasonable. It is unreasonable, however, to require all men to feel guilt for the same cause most women do. Nature is not fair. We're the ones who are unreasonable. Anyway, a bad feeling is a fair price to pay for a larger than average slice of the cake. Even though the "sensitizing" of the male requires him to feel maternally toward his babes, and would like him to feel labor too and to lactate, he can never "have" children the way a woman can, and to expect him to behave as though he can is one of monogamy's newer futilities.

Once a human father's seed has been planted, his role becomes voluntary. The transformation into father must be made in his mind; he has no other internal organ, no breasts, no special hormones to help him. His sexual apparatus, useful though it is, does not double for extra duties the way hers does, so efficiently she cannot always be sure what is primary and what is secondary to them. Some men find it distressing, even impossible, to adjust their thinking to fatherhood, especially since all its early requirements restrict freedom and access to their spouses, whose attitude to sex and life has probably been profoundly changed.

It is a current ideal to imagine that the arrival of any decent fellow's baby will turn him into a happy house-husband and nursery-hand. The truth is it may just barely turn him into a father. Babies as a rule do not interest men very much. (If they don't interest a lot of women either, they are nevertheless the price a woman pays for having them.) Marriage is an invention that constrains a man to stay around and feed his progeny, as many other males in nature do instinctively for a season or two. Though pride in his mate and children can make a man happy to do his duty, only his sense of fairness will make him pleased to sacrifice his ambition and worldly life to his young.

Certainly, in a society that advocates breastfeeding, infants must remain largely woman's work. Moreover, a man's sense of fairness may not be inclined as hers; his judgment may be that his wife is already devoting more than enough attention to the baby; it may remind him that tender, smelly, mindless nursery duties were never one of the things he wanted from life, and if she wanted them, well, that's her lookout; it may whisper he only helped her have a baby because she wanted it; it may say to him he was tricked or trapped (perhaps he was). Then again, there are men who melt at the sight of their progeny and happily tiptoe away from their sleeping wives to enjoy the pleasure of the four o'clock feed. There will always be men delighted to undertake cooking, cleaning, and nursing itself, even to excel at them; however, this is a conscious decision for the male, seen as an act of generosity or a pain in the neck by his wife, depending upon her expectations.

In many societies, children haven't much to do with their fathers until they are around seven, and then it's only boys who are removed from the nursery to live with the men in special tribal huts, or Eton, as the case may be. There used to be lessons beyond how to pee standing up that boys were expected to learn from adult men, and attitudes they could not be taught by women, for whom love, contentment and peace are more to be sought than power, struggle and fame. Now, women are beginning to say they want equality with men, only on no account do they want rivalry; they want support and house-husbands, while they detest dependency. The male is temperamentally and physically predisposed to make rivals and dependents, however; and to make them with honor was the old, heroic lesson of fathers to sons. As we put increasing priority on feminine feelings and complaints, the masculine heroic romance hardly seems worth teaching; on the contrary, it has become despicable in some circles because of its freedom from feminine controls. Very often, where a father dreamed of instructing his sons, he can only disapprove, and where he hoped to be his sons' hero, he has been replaced by pop idols and sportsmen who seem to have found a route out of anonymity, less drab and henpecked than Daddy's way. (The very same idols are pinned up over girls' beds too, except that there they serve as sex objects.) Unless a man is in one of the archaic manual professions, or is a criminal or a king, he has nothing special to demonstrate to his sons anymore, no matter how many diapers he pinned, or bottles he warmed.

The fathers of sons are redundant in a new way. Even the facts of a male's sex life will probably be taught at school, frequently by a woman to a mixed class, with emphasis on contraception, responsibility, and meaningful relationships that leave boys alone with the puzzle of their nighttime emissions, spontaneous erections, persistent wicked randiness, and wild masturbation. Fathers are being ousted from their sons' sex education, and women are increasingly in control of it. The discrepancy of interests between generations of the male sex has probably never been so great as it is now. Many men find themselves close to their sons only while they support the same football team, and a son can become an expensive reproach to his dad, a reminder that the trail he blazed is overgrown with failure and disappointment. Mothers, on the other hand, whether they get on well with their growing daughters or not, know perfectly well what girls have always been about. Attractive single mothers are starting to find the problem with adolescent daughters is that one household cannot contain comfortably the romance of two women.

It has always seemed to me that fathers, willy-nilly, exercise a passive influence on their daughters even now more telling than any active influence they hoped to exercise on sons. People worry a lot about the absence of a "role model" for the son of a single mother, like mine, but when it comes down to it, society and nature instruct both sexes in most of what they have to do, and the only thing they must learn is to whom they are doing it. Even though a son may learn from his mother, for good or ill, the manner in which he is bound to show love to women, under normal circumstances (and the majority of circumstances are normal), loving will not be as central to his life as it will to his sister's life. A mother's influence on a son is strong, but it doesn't teach him nearly as much about the main issues of his existence as he learns in the rugged, competitive playground. On this topic, however, I confess to prejudice: I have been a man's daughter and it seems to me that even the most independent girl cannot resist her father's influence successfully. There is no fighting it.

My father was a handsome man and convinced of male superiority. He was not, however, sure of its function: To instruct? But in what? To control? But whom? To set an example? To what end? Nevertheless, he knew the right of maleness to prevail was a law as mighty as those his forebears brought down from the mountain. In my father's book, three words of the Fifth Commandment—"Respect your father . . ."—were written large, with a codicil concerning the female's respect for the male. The other Commandments against adultery, theft, murder, and so on, were suitable only to exotic tribes more primitive than ours. If my father coveted anything it was what appeared to be obedience in other men's families to the great Commandment broken so routinely in his own.

"Respect! Respect!" he used to cry, and when I'd say, "Yes, but if I respect you simply for being my father, then what's that but self-love?" he'd look up to heaven and say, "You see? I get no respect!"

Correctly, he knew respect was one dynamic of a woman's love, and so when I asked why I should respect him, he heard me asking why I should love him.

I was impatient in those days, and remorselessly rational. I hurt my father because I could accept nothing without analyzing it, and give nothing without explaining too much. He was afraid of Christians, so my little successes in their world thrilled him, and at the same time, worried him. Each step I took was away from everything he felt beyond words or rationale was just, right, eternal. My new manners frightened him, and his ancient ways were a misery to me because they brought him rebuffs that made me ache with rage and tenderness. I loved him terribly, with the protective passion of a mother; it was a feeling that warred with my sanity. I found him moving, wonderful, and infuriating. He and I fought. Sometimes I pulled him word by word to common sense from a position that was illogical and, as I saw it, patently stupid. We fought about racial prejudice, we fought about privacy, we fought about the "church music" I listened to in my room behind a closed door that he feared and hated, we fought about food, about hope, about courtesy, we fought in a lather over our exasperating love for each other; and we fought about my refusal, my real inability, to submit. Our battles were genuine. Often they ended in silence when he would kill me a little by refusing to speak to me at table or to recognize my presence in the house. These tiny murders could last for days until I begged to be brought back to life by his attention and his love. Sometimes, he conceded me a point; then, always, lo and behold, like a mythological boulder, within minutes of my triumph, he had slipped back to the beginning again.

I was a city girl by birth and inclination. My father was somehow a countryman with skills I didn't understand or appreciate. He touched a melon and knew if it was ripe; he kept bees; he built boats and swings; he had a beautiful singing voice and an ear so true, my warbling must have caused him physical distress. Also, my father was superstitious. He knew any untested, adventurous move must attract the attention of malign forces and bring down the holocaust. After events in world history during my childhood appeared to prove him right, he was never again by my reckoning altogether reasonable; thereafter, he saw each daily routine as a way to propitiate supernatural evil, so any deviation even as insignificant as a detour from our familiar route to the country, or an unknown brand of tinned vegetable in the larder, or a new neighbor, was enough to make him confused and wrathful, like a priest whose rites have been interrupted by vandals.

"Dad has lost his capacity to be surprised by anything your sister does," my mother wrote in a letter my brother showed me soon after the unconventional birth of my son.

More than anything, my father hated change or surprise. In contrast, not only have I never been happy for long without them both, I have never been able to understand how anyone else can be. He was inflexible, and I was intolerant.

"No man will ever love you," my father said to me once.

He said it in sorrow. It wasn't a curse, it was a prophecy. Fathers don't curse, they disinherit. Mothers curse. In the way my father meant it, no man has ever loved me, and I've loved men in precisely the way he was afraid I would, precisely the way I loved him: passionately, out of all proportion, and always with my rational mind astounded at what it could not help. I've loved a lot of men since my father, and never one of them for a good reason. There was a time I thought his wrongheadedness would be the death of me. Now I see that whether my father was wrong in my estimation did not detract from his noble, agonizing fidelity to precepts, outmoded though they were, from which I too received all my reason and my life. His love was unshakable. He was the most faithful man a woman could ever have. Fighting all the way, he never once abandoned me, not even when I caused him pain. In the long run, my father was the making of me. Without him, I could have become the daughter he wanted.

The relationship between father and daughter belies the truism that "all men want just one thing from all women." The male's relationship to his daughter is not distorted by lust. At the same time it is a true sexual relationship. He is the hero into whose care has been given an utterly ignorant female. She was born to respect him, she is his; and what's more, unlike her mother, she is a virgin. Men are in awe of virgins while at the same time suspecting them of untapped libidinous depths. This makes a perfect condition for worship, requiring both self-denial and devotion. His daughter is a pure container of all the female magic, and he is dutybound to protect her from brutal knowledge that must come in due course through the agency of another male, a selfish one who cannot love her as her father does, or so it seems to the older male, because if he did, he could not despoil her. Some fathers are made so shy by the strength of their emotion, they fear it must be erotic (they, too, have been told through the ages they want just one thing from a female), and so they retreat from it, and from the girl. This is a sad loss for both of them because the sole true mystery of fathering is a man's singular entitlement to his daughter's trust.

Several years ago, I researched and wrote a long essay on incest. The editor who had commissioned it lost her nerve at the last minute, and withdrew it from publication. Since then, incest has become the latest of those "last taboos" to titillate the public with a deluge of words that speak the unspeakable. Most of the incest I tracked down for my story took place between siblings and seemed to do very little harm. The partners I spoke to were of much the same age, no coercion was involved, and in more than half the cases a slightly older sister had been the instigator. What is being broadcast now, however, in advice columns and regularly in dramatized documentaries as well as daily papers, is always father-daughter incest. Social horrors revealed by the media send a pleasant shiver through the community, and our prurient interest in incest as a facet of male "brutality" has probably made a balanced man or two frightened of his deep feelings toward his baby girl. It has also no doubt helped more than one daughter remember falsely that her father was responsible for her autonomous pubescent sexual stirring. Memory is a very bad housekeeper. Even Freud discovered, though predisposed not to, that out of the brew of respect, desire, and that first, unexpected, spontaneous heat, a woman can distill an attempt on her purity that never actually took place. Wherever there are two sexes, there must be sexual curiosity, and species that can't recognize their own offspring probably get around to screwing them in due course. However, humans can contain curiosity where it is ill-advised, forbidden, even deadly; men do recognize their daughters, and daughters their fathers. Whether father-daughter incest is unnatural or not is open to question; however, in our society it is certainly impolitic, and few fathers are mad or stupid enough to misinterpret at such cost the rehearsal for all future flirtations their daughters practice on them, or to fall for their fledglings' techniques of male entrapment.

Some wishful-thinking people are trying to lobotomize mankind, cut away a chunk of the subconscious, remove nature's imperatives, and rewrite even nursery tales rooted in prehistory. "Mothering" and "fathering" are to be seen as interchangeable functions and replaced by "parenting," despite evidence children have in their own homes (and in the subtle tickling of their small bodies) that it is patently untrue. Neither sex is a deformed or handicapped version of the other. Mothering is a vocation, and fathering is an act, first, of spontaneity, then, of generosity. Women have babies and thereafter must mother them for a time; men father babies and thereafter it is up to them to love them, or leave them alone.

5

THE BODY

Even a visitor from Venus or Jupiter would have to notice right away that there are major physical differences between the sexes, and the alien would probably expect behavioral differences as a result. At first sight, the average human male is bigger, hairier, flatter but not fatter, and stronger than his female counterpart. Though she can pick up hotter plates than he can, he is generally more streamlined except for one small detail: his main sex organ is external and, because he will stand upright, it is a prime target, located on a part of his body easily accessible to an aggressor's boot. Considering the vulnerability of the male organ, it astonishes me that of the hundreds of males I have met in the many countries where I have worked and traveled, I've never, so far as I know, encountered a genuine castrato, though I must say I've met a few fair facsimiles. Only a small number of the men I've known in my lifetime have not been in one kind of brawl or another, so I assume that males never attack each other's sex organs except, maybe, in a fight to the death. I've read that Etruscan soldiers used to include full erection visible under their battle dress to strike terror into their opponents' souls; how many foolhardy Etruscans left the field in mint condition, however, is not known. Is there an unwritten stricture in Mantalk against all below-the-belt combat? If so, it does not apply to women, who are instructed by their mothers to knee a rapist in the groin—very bad advice as it happens because the male organ is a smallish moving target and when the woman misses it she enrages her attacker without in the least discouraging him. It is more effective to go for his ego. "If that were mine, I wouldn't show it to anyone," a friend once said to a persistent "flasher," and sent him scurrying for cover.

When I was a little girl, I thought the major distinction between the sexes was that *they* peed standing up. At the time, that seemed an ingenious quirk, though not awfully important. Since then, I've seen many men pee outside in the open air and I've started to think there is more to the whole business than meets the eye. Be he truck driver or peer of the realm, when he takes the liberty Mother Nature grants him there is a look on his face that sends a shiver down my spine. What conceit! What hubris! To mark out territory with such careless rapture toward the distant mountains, and even under the reeking portico of Saint Peter's Basilica in Rome. How profligate a man is! How unlike a woman!

The male organ of sex, which happens also to be a channel of waste disposal, is shamanic; it is shaped for feats of strength and magic. I know a man who needs to pee in the gardens of his girlfriends before he can feel confident of his power over them. Can anyone imagine a woman staking a claim to her lover in such an unromantic way?

"Once I stood next to my girlfriend's ex-husband," he told me, "both of us pissing in a fury against her garden wall."

As a man pees, so he sees the world and so he hopes the world sees him: an upright, wide-ranging hero with his prick in his hand, his eye on the horizon and his big feet trampling the herbaceous border.

In the Arab world, desert tribesmen squat to urinate,

perhaps because their male superiority is strictly assigned
by tradition and law, so they have no need to enchant their
womenfolk or to impress each other with arcane skills. Among
us, however, the manner of male micturition is learned early
and taught preferably by an older male. The ladies' room
welcomes needy children of either sex, but the men's room
is a tabernacle sheltering the first initiation ceremony (and
is so firmly shut to females of any age that one of the most
perplexed men in Western society is a father alone at the
zoo with his baby daughter when she wants a lavatory).
Erect, competitive peeing is an important early ritual for
lads to master, and acceptance in the brotherhood requires
them to be bold and accurate in its execution. A friend of
mine who is incapable of urinating in front of other men
was considered by the examining doctor to be handicapped
to such a degree he was excused service in the United States
Army.

A boy is born with visible evidence of his sex, a tiny
plaything he can touch, stroke, and most important, compare with others; it is his very own Excalibur that will soon
perform for him in a way the little girl's tidbit of clitoris
cannot do so publicly or ostentatiously. It's hardly surprising advice columns receive letters from men who are concerned about the size of their penises: generally that they
are too small; every so often that they are too big. Women
and homosexual men frequently talk about the way their
lovers are "hung," in spite of the genteel censorship about
letting on to a heterosexual male that the size of his penis
matters. Men make bad losers and they are impotent in
defeat. The most liberated woman still wants her male
rampant, at the very least for evidence she is loved, and if
a man is dispirited or worried, particularly about his penis,
he just cannot get it up. If he cannot get it up he will, first,
be unable to make love or babies; and second, in his fear
and desperation he will probably blame his partner. A new
woman is an aphrodisiac, and so he will leave, leave, leave,

and leave again, until he is exhausted or trapped. Is it any wonder no woman will tell her lover he is too small to suit her?

Our society purports to believe female orgasm is a very good thing, and also that ideally it should occur during intercourse (certainly a lot of women complain when it doesn't); at the same time, it is put about that the size of the penis doesn't matter. Surely it takes no great understanding of physiology or physics to grant that if women are to "come" while fucking, a substantial bit of the man must be involved. Even women who don't climax during the act of intercourse itself are concerned about size because an adequate penis makes an emphatic union. Of course, there will always be some females who prefer a small, unthreatening penis and go out of their way to find one. I met a girl in Singapore who had traveled all the way from Sevenoaks on just such a quest. At some time in his life every man wonders nervously if his organ is big enough to justify his pride in it. Is he as well-equipped as other lovers his girlfriend has had? Is it true, as Mantalkers say, that all penises are the same in erection? Do uncircumcised men derive more sensation or less than others? Are black men bigger than white men? The fact of the matter is, our human male is the only creature in nature inflicted with penis envy.

As a general rule, for reasons as obvious as menstruation, childbearing, diapers and cats' litter trays, women are less fastidious than men, who prefer to live in ignorance of their own intimate physiology. As long as their penises do the job, they'd rather not know how it's done. There could hardly be a literate man left in the west who hasn't some idea where a female keeps her clitoris, and not many fathers these days escape information about the last wrinkle of the uterus, whether they want to have it or not; however, men are not often told that, for example, the angle of male erection between the ages of twenty and seventy slips from 10 percent above the horizontal to 25 percent below it. There are no magazine articles written about the male's ability to fake orgasm in order to spare a partner's feelings, or because he has a headache, or, most likely, to spare himself an emotional scene. The shelves are full of books about breast cancer, but there is less publicity about cancer of the testicles and the penis, or the high incidence of prostate cancer. (Not many men even know where their prostates are.) Women talk to each other and write relentlessly in newspapers and magazines about the menopause. Would any man's magazine dare to tell its readership that long before the age of seventy most of them will have no more sex life at all? Or that over the age of fifty-five or so a third of them will no longer be capable of strong or regular erections? And a lot of them won't give a damn, either.

"Prostatitis came as a great relief to me," a celebrated womanizer over sixty said to me once, "and the first thing I thought when I lost my virginity at sixteen was, 'Thank God that's over and done with.' " He passed his hand over the artful parting of his hair.

"Have you ever considered," he said thoughtfully, "how much of a cocksman's sex life is a valediction?"

Physical vanity, if it comes at all, comes later to males than it does to women. Most of the male's pride is in his strength rather than his beauty, and in the triumphs of his bits and brains rather than how charming they all are. Vanity in men (everything in men) is subservient to boss ego, just as in women all bows to love. Girls are cautious from the start of receiving wounds or bruises because they know perfectly well their future depends upon their appearance; not many lads, however, grow up without scars to show. In the playground where little boys exchange baby talk for the grammar of Mantalk, they soon discover how to challenge each other, what to say to other boys, and what they must never say to the darling tyrant at home who is bound to make a fuss. Recently when my son returned from a weekend with a schoolmate in the country he stood at our front door with his back to me.

"Please, don't get excited," he said before turning around to show me a gash on his upper lip. "It's not nearly so bad as it looks."

Physical force is part of contest, and contest is part of boyhood, bearing with it many lessons that later become part of manhood: not to cry out of self-pity, for example, and to save tears for those few occasions that merit them. There is more competitive rough stuff in one year of a boy's life than a female encounters in a decade because testing physical strength is a valid element of maleness, and one from which women, mistaking it always for brutality, turn their eyes. Only when males are frustrated, or villainous, or when they are mad, does their vigor go haywire and become brutal, the way it is shown to be in some abominable pornography only available in cartoon strips because the barbed wheels, serrated axes, complex pulleys, and various bloodshedding mechanisms of an unhappy imagination would leave no living survivors. These abhorrent fantasies, and the occasional monster who tries to implement them in real life (not always a man), have little to do with sex as a primary human function; they use it instead as a symbol of hatred directed not so much against the female as against life itself. Such aberrant passion is uncivilized, evident in savages and sometimes in children.

When I was a teenager I worked at an American summer camp where well-off parents paid for their offspring to live in tents, and eat junk food, and generally enjoy a life of extreme poverty. In my group was the seven-year-old son of two psychiatrists, an undersized boy whom I referred to privately as "pre-shrunk." One morning I stopped him from braining another boy with a large mallet we used to pound in tent stakes. I had to struggle with him for the weapon because his rage made him very strong, and when I finally twisted it out of his hands I saw a total absence of control or imagination in his eyes. I had been grappling with a ferocious and isolated ego: with a murderer, in fact. Such uncontrolled passion is rare among men, and usually occurs when valid, male feelings have been denied or squeezed down into a box; then, let a fracture occur, and out they come, white hot and angry.

The human adult male is potentially the most dangerous creature in existence. He is quick, he can swing a club, use a lever, squeeze a trigger. Only his physical, intellectual, and emotional controls keep him from the destruction of himself and others. For very good reason, men are proud of their control, and admire in their brothers an Oriental awareness of nothingness that cannot be learned without some experience of violence. Americans call this quality "cool." Once, at a party in a suburban garden I watched two grown men, both sober, throw penknives at each other's bare feet. All the women looked away, while the other men watched, fascinated by the test of absolute confidence and perfect control of both the knife and the emotions.

"Now, that takes balls," our host said.

When a man says another man has "balls," that is a compliment. If he calls the other "a prick," however, he is looking for a fight. Balls are a discrete, conservative power, more reliable than the penis, which is the show-off of his body: insecure, unreliable, treacherous and out of control.

Sports are a display of physical control even more than they are of strength. Young men playing sports are wholehearted, concentrating, happy; and sometimes there is a communication among teammates that is practically telepathic, fusing them into a singleness, usually in opposition to another entity at the opposite end of the playing field, or the other side of the fortifications. Healthy men are as vain of their speed and skill as women are of their beauty. One

October day on the island of Barbados I saw young men the color of Guinness stout turning cartwheels in the sun, and for the first time I understood why some homosexuals are compelled to collect boys who are at the very summit of amateurism, just before their sheer delight in being and doing gives way to responsibilities. I've known homosexual males of prestige who have ruined themselves emotionally and financially for graceful striplings like those I watched spinning on the Caribbean sand. I daresay just as many tropical ports have been ruined by commerce of that kind as by package tours or water pollution. The collector's gay concupiscence is perverse, as though he acquired fine porcelain just in order to smash it, for as soon as a male learns to set a price on his good looks, he becomes corrupt, weak and effeminate. Only a woman can use beauty as collateral for deals, and make a business of her appearance, without becoming absolutely rotten, though I cannot say I've never known a woman to be improved by such transactions.

It is often said that men are more vain of their appearance than women; however, it is only very young males, who are dying to get laid and have nothing to offer but their bodies, who spend even a fraction of the time, money, care or comfort on their appearance that every woman does. The plainest man can make females lean his way sexually with the allure of his wealth, his wit, his strength, his intentions, his position, even just his tennis backhand if it's triumphant enough. Physical vanity in a grown man is a weakness; in a woman it is an asset of maturity and a tool for one of the serious undertakings of her life: male entrapment. Pretty women have more suitors than their homely sisters, and that's a fact. The concern a woman brings to her reflection is as professional as she can make it; sometimes it is even inspired.

For a few months, I worked in a menial capacity for a famous French couturier who designed for film stars, and females in the entourages of fabulously rich men. Although I wasn't well-groomed enough to be allowed into the full light of his temple, sometimes I'd creep out of the oubliette where I worked, and from the shadows of the plush fitting rooms I watched the icy detachment of rich women testing the effect of a tuck. I've seen what a professional eye a woman can level on the power of a hemline to enhance or conceal. Their clinical appraisal was the closest thing I've ever known to pure objectivity. I don't particularly respect females who possess this gift, though I must admire their level heads that see a new dress not as a witty, irresistible confection, but rather as something integral to the gorgeous thing they are making, which happens to be themselves.

The materials a woman uses and the people she can hire to help her investment—cosmeticians, designers, dieticians, plastic surgeons, dentists, hair stylists, manicurists, leg waxers, eyelash dyers—are the best she can afford until she marries the money she is angling for and can afford better. The only men possessed of comparable physical vanity are those who require love as women do, and seek it from vast audiences. Homosexual males and a few extraordinarily tough women run the industry of beauty because they understand precisely how far women will go to satisfy male fantasies, yet they themselves remain apart from the games a client plays in the frivolities they design for her and to which, by the by, she is enslaved. There are secretaries who spend more on face creams than they do on food, and I remember a countrywoman of mine, wife of a famous statesman, who nearly caused an international scandal because she refused to "buy American" as long as the French continued to make the most clever clothes. The great gurus of fashion are aloof. There is a saint's festival in France when the designers' showrooms are closed to the public for private celebrations. It's customary for the "master," as a top couturier is known in his own "house," to present each of his mannequins with a little gift and a kiss. Our "master" stood handsome and svelte on a stage in the gold and mushroom-beige showroom to receive some of the most beautiful girls in Paris, his own clotheshorses, a lot of them bound for liaisons that would turn them into clients: kiss-kiss, kiss-kiss, kiss-kiss, a kiss for each cheek in the French style, and between each pair of kisses he raised a white linen handkerchief to pat his mouth in a gesture of noble disdain.

The craft of self-beautification allows aging women to embalm their youth in rituals, oils and unguents worthy of a dead pharaoh. It also allows special men to produce astonishing impersonations of female beauty. The French call professional transvestites *travesties*, and they have the right idea. Being a race that has raised vanity to an art form, it's to be expected the French would also produce the most glorious travesties. Not for our gay Parisians, the vulgar, flouncing send-ups of British television comics, or the besequinned "drag acts" where paunchy fellows mime to Ginger Rogers records, sometimes with an earnestness that shows they actually dream Fred Astaire will arrive to sweep them and their five-o'clock shadows off on a cloud of stars. French travesties, and those *artistes* who find their way inevitably to Frenchified parts of the globe, embody the wickedness of glamour that dazzles with false promises. The pretty boys in drag are real heartbreakers, flashing their long legs and brief costumes, bosoms padded or hothouse grown with the help of hormone injections. Once, I found myself at a club for travesties in Tangiers with a young Englishman not long out of his posh public school.

"Oh, no, no, it cannot be!" he said. "They just can't be men. They must be women!"

His despair increased as each act, more sinuous and scantily clad than the last, wriggled and writhed across the stage. By the end of the evening, he was nearly in tears.

"I don't believe it," he kept saying. "They have to be women. Please tell me they're women!"

All the boys, none of them much older than he, had been impersonating a young man's dream of the outrageous, the inaccessible, the glittering and dangerous divine. Their disguises were sensational, until we were invited backstage and the gorgeous creature talking to us lifted his wig. At one blow the looking glass cracked to show us the face of the demimonde painted with vanity and lust, half-masked, and absolutely depraved.

"Mirror, mirror on the wall," challenges the travesty, with confidence only a few goddesses of the silver screen have ever found in their female souls. It is the impersonator's confident perfection that is his flaw; no real woman ever feels entirely beautiful until she is safely loved by a man, the very one she has created herself to complement. In the end, the best female impersonators will always have been women.

Physical vanity is a characteristic of little girls and women in their prime, and it makes a male effeminate, whether he's an epicene pop star or a catamite cruising the gay bars. Any creature truly vain of appearance must be too self-conscious for uninhibited, bruising, vigorous physical activity. Even among women, I have often had the impression that the greater her vanity, the less chance she will lend herself to the hurly burly of sexual passion, which demands, at its best, suspension of self-consciousness.

"The only part of sex I really enjoy," a beautiful woman once told me, "is the look in a man's eyes the first time he sees me with my clothes off."

No man could ever make such a statement for many reasons, one of them that vanity is a lonesome little vice, setting itself apart from other people and from action. Vanity finds confidence in acts of self-devotion before a mirror. A man, on the other hand, is most secure and happy when he is one of a pack. Whether it's a Brooks Brothers suit, a judge's robes, or a green pricklebacked lizard on his scalp, the male is most at ease when he's wearing a uniform.

6
STATUS

When I was a child, our holiday home in the mountains was a clapboard house with a porch, an artesian well, and hornets' nests in the attic. Day for day, I spent less time there than I did in our city flat, but I remember it nevertheless as the house where I grew up. With my mind's eye I can still see every hillock and ripple on the big lawn where my brother and I played savage games of croquet with our gang of local kids. There were six miniature fruit trees set far apart in the grass, and at the bottom of the lawn a thicket of silver birches that was hellish to circumnavigate with ball and mallet. Behind the house was a flower garden my grandmother preferred to children, and guarded with the insomnious temper of Cerberus.

My parents bought the place when I was barely five and over the years they added to the land around it, finally buying a plot across the narrow dirt road that fronted on the lake itself. This was a source of wonders, snakes and islets; the stumps of a drowned forest stood above water level, hiding catfish that came up on our hooks, croaking like heavy smokers. We pulled our canoes ashore on damp, brown beaches to play pirates, and there was one bridge where huge, black spiders lay doggo on the struts overhead as we slipped under them. In my memory, one summer flows into the next like streaks of fool's gold in the rocks my brother and I collected to trade with our friends.

Then, the year I turned fourteen and my brother was eleven, the idyll went the way of all good things, and bad ones too. Our gang, roughly the same age, over the winter had started to divide into girls and boys. Even my best friend, only a year older than I, had taken to worrying about her hair and the straps on her swimsuit. There were hot days when she didn't want to swim at all anymore, only to sit watching the rest of us with a dreamy and somehow superior smile. The girls went silly first. They lost interest in the blueberry bunkers where we had gathered the wild harvest every summer of our lives. They couldn't be enticed to follow the trees that had been bent as saplings by Appalachian Indians to mark the ancient trails. They preferred to whisper together, or run squealing along the "Big Beach" where the older boys, not ever part of our gang, were playing ball. Some of those boys already had cars of their own. They used to waste beautiful summer days on their backs under them, shouting to each other about things like carburetors.

Then, I found out the boys in my old gang had formed a club of their own with a secret meeting place in the woods, and handshakes, and a code, and all sorts of things with "no girls allowed," my brother said. Soon the older boys, who were still too young to drive cars, had licenses for speedboats that chopped the lake and littered the shore with dead sunfish. Everyone was talking about Evinrudes and Mercurys, and for the first time our canoe spent the summer suspended in its hammock over my father's car in the garage. It didn't matter anymore to me. I'd taken to sitting on the shady side of the house reading poetry and suffering. By the time I understood the girls better I was too sunk in melancholy to join them, and my brother had his own Mercury Super Ten outboard motor on a real boat, not one built by our father.

What was more, when he zoomed back and forth across the lake (my sea of mysteries, grown suddenly very small), he wore a yachting cap.

The male's insatiable appetite for secret societies, jargons and expensive, licensed machines is puzzling to women whose initiation ceremonies and stages of growth are marked by biology. Female puberty begins with a flourish, and from then on all the stages of her physical maturity and sisterhood are dramatically marked. Males, in the meantime, are going through physical transitions that are not traumatic at the time, whatever anguish they cause later. A boy's voice cracks and he hops from the angelic choir into the randy hoard; his sex organ grows and he waits in eager terror to use it. He becomes a man, yet he doesn't bleed, ache, labor or give birth, and strictly speaking he isn't deflowered or invaded by sex, no seal in him is broken; with his first sex act he gains more than he loses.

The male ego is therefore compelled to invent mutual, shared ways men can assure themselves and indicate to others that their progress is normal, they are not alone, and they have not failed. Life for a man is a series of bar mitzvahs, and because these rites of passage are mankind's own inventions, he is able to persuade himself of his maturity only by persuading others of it first. Thus men clamber for rank, symbols and insignia to show off their position in the male hierarchy or, more likely, to show others where they fancy themselves worthy of being. They inherit rank rather than prospects, they drive symbols instead of cars, they wear insignia, not clothes. In a man's world, to own the best is to be seen as being the best, and to take a chance on anything at all that is odd or out of the ordinary is to risk failure and derision.

The human male is an orthodox creature conventional in his tastes, and all conventions except romantic monogamy aggrandize him. When a man dares to be unconventional he makes a go of it only if other men follow him, incidentally attracting women to the camp of, say, Marxism, Calvinism, Freudianism, Mohammedanism, or good old Christianity. It is not equally difficult for a woman to be unconventional with impunity because she is a smaller threat to the status quo. Nobody will follow her into rebellion except perhaps a few other women, and even fewer men. This can make her free. Inside my own family, for instance, as inside bigger society, it was easier for me to accomplish a personal rebellion, to become an expatriate, to follow my dodgy path, than it would have been for my brother-the-doctor had he been tempted to (which, indeed, he was) because everyone assumed sooner or later love was going to tame me, and therefore nobody took me very seriously. All I had to do was liberate myself from my own fear of not being loved (or make the fear work for me, the way it does for an actress who courts an audience). My brother-the-doctor, however, in order to become my brother-the-sailor or my brother-the-historian, would have needed to free himself from a fear that pervades every area of a male's life and has been, in its own way, the dynamic of our society: fear of failing. When a man is courageous enough to become an eccentric, a rebel, an artist, he stands to be one of the most magnificent successes in human history precisely because the odds are so much against him and the risks incalculably great. The fortitude he needs is nearly superhuman.

"I think you're brave to do it," I told a man who is by trade a deep-sea diver and by inclination an artist.

"Just imagine," he replied, "what I'm so afraid of, I'd rather be a diver."

Men are the suckers. One way or another, practically all advertising is on behalf of the masculine image, either showing him what kind of status he can hope to attain, or showing a woman what kind of man she can hope to attract. Advertising addressed to women always promises love: someone wonderful will canter up on a white horse if she uses the right soap, her husband will never leave her if she gives him the right coffee, and if she wears the swimsuit on page 98, she will magnetize muscular males like those who are prowling around the model in the photograph. Advertising aimed at men promises that if he buys the right razor he will be as daring as hang gliders who carouse with the wind; if he drinks one brand of vodka, he will be among the rich smoothies who frequent the best hotels in Europe, if he drinks another, he will be as strong as a famous butch movie actor; if he buys the right car, he will pull birds and also, it goes without saying, his erection will never wilt. Advertising demeans men. It turns their heroic longings for triumph, freedom, and elemental sex into four wheels, a floozy, and a Havana cigar.

A man sets out to package himself in a manner that can identify a true hero; however, more often he only manages to show who his hero is. Possibly the most important item in the masculine collection of status symbols is a car. His car may turn out to be the biggest thing he buys in his lifetime except for a house, and that he makes over, more or less, to his wife and children. I've met men who cannot remember the names of the women they've had in bed, yet they can recall the smallest quirk and tremor of every vehicle they have ever possessed right back to their two-wheeler bike; and the first car is always tender in their memory as the sweetheart who made them potent, bold, and independent at last of nursery rule. There is a common notion that men see their automobiles as extensions of their penises. I, however, am not persuaded this is so. For one thing, I've never met a man who called his car by any but the feminine pronoun, sometimes even referring to "her" as "baby," the way Humphrey Bogart did Lauren Bacall.

I am pretty sure a man's motorcar doesn't symbolize his male part; on the contrary, I think it represents his fantasy female. No matter what model he drives, he dreams of the one he'd love to be handling, the one he'd like all his friends to see leaping at his touch: a fast Italian, maybe, or a big, strong Swede, a dependable German with good lines, a long, flash Yankee (expensive to fuel), the cuddly little car next door, or even a vintage vehicle of high style and lots of experience, old enough to be grateful for his attention. Furthermore, there is a vast difference between the cars a man drives before and after marriage: premarital cars are carefree, raffish—mothers do not approve of them; postmarital cars are responsible and roomy. Men who can afford the luxury keep a marital car in the garage and drive something racier in town.

Without money a man is helpless; he cannot invent himself or acquire any of the symbols of status. If he is poor, he must depend for his image on the charity of others, and this is a greater humiliation for a man than for his nursery-educated sister who takes courtesy and "reverse discrimination" as her due, and even complains that men are chauvinistic when she doesn't get them (and just as chauvinistic when she does). Money and hair are the two power symbols men worry about losing, and money is the symbol of symbols. Being a semblance of power, money can even buy a semblance of love. Any run-of-the-mill millionaire can get laid more easily than a common pauper. Females find money sexy. It's understandable that the verb "to spend" has a sexual connotation.

In glamorous places where men go to gamble, the call girl is offered as make-believe booty of the make-believe warrior-king. She'll help him pretend he's Attila the Honeybun, no courtship or commitment needed, only a few hundred dollars of his resources. A fine understanding of male ego is found in brochures handed out in the hotels and casinos of Las Vegas to the suckers who come there to make heroic whoopee.

"The most expensive Escort Service in Las Vegas: we represent a glittering array of the most highly preferred companions of distinction, carefully screened for gentlemen of discriminating taste. . . ."

"If you're the King of Diamonds, I'll be your Queen of Hearts. Call Bernadine. . . . Visa and Mastercard accepted. . . ."

No emotions to unman him, nothing more than he can spare, and he can't make a mistake. All he needs is his heroic imagination and a credit rating. If by chance the sucker cannot get an erection, she'll tell him anyway he's the best she's ever had because that's what he's paying for; and if he doesn't believe her, what the hell? She's only a hooker. Moreover, she's pretty as the showgirl she went to Vegas to be, and she's disease-free, which is more than can be said for a lot of amateurs. She really is the best money can buy for a night. A man who can afford to do it deserves to take his ease with such a creature. She'll murmur "lover" for a while, and when he's gone, she'll call him "a john," "a sucker," "a trick." He'll probably call her a business expense.

Men manage to be both extravagant and mean. They will spend lavishly to enhance their own images, but not on much else; thus, nine times out of ten when a man is altruistic it's a tax dodge. Maybe it has been just my luck to attract misers; certainly, a lot of men have cried into beer from my fridge about how much money they've spent on other women. One ex-lover, who used me as an unpaid babysitter for his adolescent offspring, told me he had bought my predecessor a three-week tour of India so the heat could help her chronic backache. Incidentally, I must add, he'd been keen to see the last of that aching back. When she returned from her free trip she found herself moved out of his flat and replaced by the next woman in his life. (All I gained materially after that fling was a corkscrew that has never worked. I should have made it worth more to get rid of me.) Men give nothing away, especially money, unless they are going to get something in return: freedom, a status symbol, a fuck. Women, on the other hand, are rarely equally crass, because they are desirous of love more than status. They contrive charming gifts for friends and menfolk. A woman I knew in New York designed a birthday present of extraordinary complexity, involving helium-filled balloons, a Cartier watch, two kosher salamis, and an orthodox rabbi to deliver it to her lover's door. Just three weeks later, the affair was over.

"All that time and money on the bastard's gift, too," I said to her.

"I don't regret it," she said, sniffing and wiping away a tear. "If he didn't love me for that, he was never going to love me."

Except in perverse circles where poverty itself is a symbol of goodness and more prestige is attached to writing a poem than writing a check for two million, money is the sturdiest of props to male ego. I've had men friends tell me tales about their sex lives who could not bring themselves to reveal their annual income because that would be too personal, too specific, and too easy to compare. When bankrupts hurled themselves from skyscrapers during the Great Depression, dropping on Wall Street like apples under trees, they did it because they found themselves suddenly without status, without symbols, without secrets; they found themselves naked, and they died of shame. Personally, I've never met a rich man I've liked. I admit, however, that rich men do not find me attractive, so perhaps my judgment is colored. Ages ago, I was interviewed by a filthy-rich American for a job on a magazine he owned. Even then, twenty dollars a week was not a living wage. As I sat in his luxurious hotel suite debating with myself whether a job was worth any price to me, even starvation, the door flew open and a girl of about my own age entered in a flurry of fur and perfume.

"Darling," she said to my interviewer, "I'm depressed."

He reached into his pocket, and from a pigskin wallet he drew out a hundred-dollar bill. I'd never seen one before.

"Here you go, chicken," he said, "buy yourself a pair of shoes."

Me, he was offering twenty dollars a week. Her? Fifty dollars a foot. Of course, she was doing more for his image than I could ever do; I was merely being asked to do a little something for his magazine. Even the quality of her wardrobe was a compliment to his taste in women, while the wittiest words I could write might very well turn out to insult him. I would probably outlast her in the long run. Nevertheless, one thing was certain—no doorman was ever going to walk my borzois in Central Park while I spent the day shopping for shoes on Madison Avenue.

"What do you think of her?" a man with a taste for motorbikes and black leather asked me after I'd met his newest girlfriend.

"She's crazy about you," I said.

He stretched and smiled.

"You think so? How can you tell?"

"Nobody would wear heels that high," I said, "unless she was madly in love."

Males are goofy for packaging. Because they genuinely respond sexually to an image, they believe the image must be the real McCoy. Women understand this male weakness perfectly and use it to their own advantage. The woman teetering beside a man, or behind him, is an accessory after the fact of his maleness, and that is a role she has designed herself to play, with the help of her mother and other experts. Even when a few of my university friends and I gave up makeup and began to dress exclusively in blue jeans and pullovers, we were not sending out a message of man-hating celibacy; on the contrary, the information we transmitted (with about as much success as the *Titanic* S.O.S.) was that we wanted sensitive, intelligent men to be attracted to our honest, inner selves and not just to how tight our jeans happened to be over nice young hips and bottoms. It is thanks to male susceptibility that blondes, particularly bleached blondes, have more fun, and also, that it is unusual to find one as "chairperson" of any board of directors. Men never learn that the wrapping is not supposed to reflect the contents, but to disguise them. When a man sees a woman wobbling on stiletto heels, he knows, first, that she does not intend to run away; then, when she flashes intimate bits of her anatomy or her wardrobe, he immediately thinks she must be panting for a fuck, and so he ceases on the spot to be afraid of failure or rejection. Because the poor sucker flatters himself such a hot number must want body just the way he does, free and clear of heart or soul, he starts to feel horny; she, however, is thinking all the time woman-like that sex is love. It could even be that the more overtly sexy a female makes herself appear to be, the less she actually enjoys sex. It is love, for which sex is merely a metaphor, her mink-fringed eyes beseech of each new partner; it is love she needs over and over again; and what can that mean except she has never got enough of it? And that must mean she has not, in spite of all the experience she's had, been satisfied.

Man is just like all other male animals, unimaginative about the females he chooses, attracted to what looks like a sure thing. He shows more flair when choosing ties.

"You're beautiful without your glasses," breathes a near-sighted hero who is actually saying in Mantalk: "Women who wear glasses read books, and women who read books are trouble."

There are some who would claim a genetic imperative is at work and men never make passes at girls who wear glasses because that means they have a defective chromosome; I suspect the fact is a man prefers to be seen escorting a female who does not strain the credulity of his peers, and whom any of his mates can see reasons to desire. A man's woman is a living status symbol; she advertises his judgment, his sexual prowess, his politics, and his income; that is exactly what she has always expected to do, and several paces behind him is the safest place for her to be. The discarded wives and mistresses of famous men are often passed on to colleagues or competitors who would emulate the hero, pit themselves against his memory, and learn some of his secrets. Generally, women to this very day still scramble for position in their own hierarchy according to where their mates stand on the ladder; thus, the wives of eminent men lose more when they lose their husbands, even though all abandoned wives, for a while at least, think they have lost everything. A powerful woman must reverse the position; when she stands up before her audience, everyone is curious to see what kind of man puts up with her. If she is an icon of rare glamour, heterosexual males will shun her shadow, while she consoles herself with a court of gay men in their glad rags, like ladies-in-waiting around a queen. The symbols of progress and success—a car, a suitable woman, a house, a stripe, a star, a miter, a designer shirt, a key to the men's room, a scalp or two—all indicate safe progress or arrival. The man who has none of these things is seen to have failed, and a man's worldly failure is death, not just to his ego but to much more. A world in which men ceased to fear failure would be without curiosity, invention or endeavor; it would be like one of those North African countries where women get on with subsistence and childbearing while their men squat by the roadside, smoking hashish and letting moments melt into lifetimes that leave history unmarked. When men fail, everyone fails.

7
WORK

The resources of our planet are controlled by
men. Men also control each other; with less
success they control themselves; and with least success of
all they try to control Nature, who is like a Victorian matron: bind her in one place, and she has to swell in another.
Men have been perfecting rules and disciplines for their
control of absolutely everything since time began; it is the
only way they can keep the upper hand on sloth, chaos,
brutality and madness, to say nothing of disease, starvation,
and women. All this control demands a price, and it's true
that our society is shot through with neuroses. (Those who
long for the good old days, however, forget that very few
of us now die in childbirth or are burned at the stake.) The
system of running the world is loosely divided into areas
such as government, agriculture, communications, building
and demolition, transport, education, science, and finance.
To keep the massive undertaking of universal control going
smoothly, maintaining and designing sophisticated tools has
itself become a profession and discipline.

The business of controlling all the controls is a super-
structure on survival. Its base is lost in the mud and its upper
turrets are hidden in clouds of ambition. Most men work
to preserve some part of the towering, intricate construc-

tion; though they never even see the whole, they spend their lifetimes performing abstract routines on its behalf, and for this they earn the greatest abstract of all: money. A millionaire, for example, can live in luxury without ever carrying a penny in his pocket; the owner of a chain of supermarkets would probably starve if he found himself stranded on a desert island. Very few men actually partake of what they help produce: builders raise walls for strangers, doctors die; accountants sometimes go bankrupt. The fantasy of returning to nature, where to make a killing meant to feed the tribe and be rewarded with the juiciest tidbits and the prettiest girls, is a dream for men stuck in early morning traffic on the highways. Working to no end but money would be abject slavery, hardly more understandable than a treadmill, if men had not learned how to turn their jobs into dangerous, complicated, competitive, and sometimes addictive games: imitations of war and brute survival quite like the games they learned as boys in the playground. The most successful men in any field are those who bend the rules, take the ball and run, kick competitors in the teeth and live for the sport, finding it worth the candle that burns later and later into the night, casting light on their increasingly complex schemes. The most competitive and single-minded male gets to the top, runs the show, makes policies, and wins the laurels. It's a boy's world.

The games of commerce and government look like fun. Women want to play, too. However, not all men like women on their playing fields. For one thing, they are honestly afraid they will hurt those they feel a real duty to protect. For another, the workplace may be the only place where a lot of them can escape the complaints, insecurities and nagging of their wives. Finally, women do not understand that to keep the planet rolling is a task that can be accomplished only in the spirit of the arena. Anything except whining goes as long as it works. It doesn't matter how many women become stockbrokers; they will achieve mastery of finance only when one or two women are imprisoned for embezzlement on a grand scale. For the most part, women do not enter into the state of play. They are too earnest in the field and that makes trouble for everyone. Earnest people are those who are not feeling spontaneously what they think they ought to feel; earnest people are pretending, and are therefore not trustworthy. The earnestness of women at work springs from a genuine conflict: power is the aim of the game and they know they ought to shoot for it; at the same time, power makes women unlovable and that is a price few of them can bear to pay.

An ambitious man needs to find something to do in life; an ambitious woman, however, needs to find something else to do. From this difference springs the dilemma that predisposes the modern female to neurosis and dilettantism. Because of romantic longing for love, and a maternal inclination, simply because she *can* do something other than compete with men for money or status, the female is possessed of a greater potential for regret than the male, and a smaller one for satisfaction. Hairline cracks in the feminine ego are prone to fracture. Do what she will, a part of her wonders what it would be like to have done the other thing; and if she tries to do both things at once, she will dream of how much more she could do for either, if it weren't for the other. She can have one achievement only by denying another or by compromise, which is never compatible with real, egocentric, driving, triumphant ambition. Now that a woman has more choices than ever, she has more reason for complaint; particularly if she mistook being able to choose for being able to have it all. Her history of caring for others while at the same time taking no responsibility for herself has instilled in her a need to blame, and more often than not, the one she blames is a man. It isn't even unusual nowadays to hear a woman blame the whole of malekind for her failure to achieve goals she never came near, not just because many men don't like women in their playground, but also because she was afraid of making herself unlovable by trying, or because she waited for a man to hand her the bull's-eye on a plate. Or because she actually was not very good at her job.

When a man triumphs and gets to the top of his heap, he becomes the idol of other men and even though the big boss is often uncommonly ugly, he is desired by pretty women. When a woman succeeds in the wide world, however, she pays a price.

"I'd trade every word I've ever written," a prize-winning woman novelist told me, "for a husband and children."

The only man who would need to consider a similar choice is one who has been called to the priesthood. A woman not satisfied to dabble, who makes a real, going career outside home and family, must find a devotion that is nearly religious if she is ever to achieve the wholeheartedness necessary for success, and give up without blame or regret the traditional comforts of a female's life. Meanwhile, her brother, from the starting gun, has mind and body in concert; success for him on the one hand does not entail failure or even compromise on the other, as in the end it always does for a woman. The moment a female strides into the arena looking to make a name for herself, she becomes less desirable. In Mantalk she becomes a "ball-breaker." Even when she wins for herself, all by herself, the alluring accessories with which a successful man decorates his wife or mistress, her suitors become fewer. The woman of attainment clearly doesn't need a man for anything he can give in the self-aggrandizing way men prefer to give, so if she needs a man at all, it must be for dangerous services: as a body slave, which is degrading for him, or to star in the reforming feminine romance that threatens to curtail his freedom. Her expertise, celebrity, money, intel-

ligence, even her rare beauty, reduces the field of men she
can respect and empties it of those who would presume to
adore her. Only a crazed rapist would trust himself to fuck
her. This is truly at the heart of arguments against higher
education for women: it makes them less desirable.

The soft, unformed areas of a woman's persona flatter a
man. The more independent she is, the less she appears to
need him, and the more she threatens to humiliate him. A
brilliant woman executive, say, lonesome for a mate, has
very few choices. She could flirt with a colleague of equal
standing except that from the moment they met, she would
be challenging him with competition and possible failure in
what he sees as a war game; failure at a woman's hand, no
less. There are soldiers who would kill themselves rather
than risk such disgrace. Were she to find an eminent man
from some discipline other than her own, he wouldn't understand her disposal of time and energy, or the importance
of her work in the scheme of things. For that matter, she
wouldn't understand his. I recently heard a successful bar-
rister and avowed male feminist describe his perfect "equal"
mate as someone who "shares my joys, my triumphs, my
frustrations: a friend." What about her joys and triumphs
and frustrations? Who is going to be her friend? A successful
woman can always find a superior in terms, at least, of
income and power; however, any male superior to a woman
as gifted as she is, is also superior to seven eighths of womankind. He can pick among countless nubile, flattering females. He doesn't need a challenge. At his position in life,
hasn't he earned the right to a little heroic relaxation?

A woman I know who runs an upmarket dating bureau
in Washington that matches female surgeons to male big-
game hunters, or vice versa, told me that after a magazine
published the incomes and marital status of America's fifty
richest men, she was inundated with requests for dates,
not from gold diggers in the ordinary sense, rather from

high-flying, high-earning women who wanted their mates to dominate their incomes, at least. One of them, a corporate lawyer, said she desired a self-made man so she could "instruct him in a tasteful way to spend his money." Not one of the men, when approached, was at all interested. Either they were too busy for dalliance, or they had their beds full of starlets and models.

"Generally, it's practically impossible," my acquaintance said, "to find quality dates for even the most attractive career women who are over forty."

Out of loneliness and frustration, the extraordinary woman can be driven to a man so much her junior, or so much her inferior in status or intelligence, he is flattered that she allows him to worship her. At least, he's flattered until he realizes how terrified she is of not being loved, how much she needs him, and how much power he has over her; then, that table turns sharply. Much has been written recently about famous, glamorous old women setting up house with pretty boys. When interviewed, they usually say their love has transcended the age barrier. The fact of the matter is, however, that a kid is often the best a geriatric Juliet can find because all the tough old Romeos are jigging with moppets at the disco—or, maybe, writing their masterpieces in tax havens with a sweet girl on call when they want her.

The first boss I ever worked for was a woman, personnel director of a high-fashion department store that was run by another woman, it happened, whose staff was mostly female. My direct superior was married, unlike the other women executives in the place, and a lot of the training I received from her turned out to be in housewifery: I took hubby's suits to the cleaners (with a request to pay particular attention to the wine stains). I had his tennis racquet restrung where he appeared to have smashed it on a post. I shopped for his chops, and asked the butcher to trim all fat from them because our husband was worried about cholesterol.

It never entered my mind to resent these homely chores, the way my predecessor had done until the day she quit. Just as my boss was in awe of the great career woman in charge of us all, so I was in awe of everyone, and avid to show my gratitude for employment. What's more, my boss was the fair-haired girl of the moment, climbing the ladder steadily. Within six months of my arrival she had been given a big raise in pay and high-pile beige carpet in her office. Almost immediately afterward, her husband left us. Were we sorry to be rid of him? Not in the least.

"He was never very much," she told me in a moment of rare confidence. "I should have done better, but I wasn't so hip as I am now."

For a little while, instead of lean meat I was sent out for champagne, pâtés, cut roses, and all that was necessary for the intimate dinners of a woman on the way up. My boss bought a blue fox coat, and on Mondays she spent an hour with the same psychiatrist the great career woman consulted on Wednesdays and Fridays. (I rarely saw our top woman except sometimes in the "ladies" when she raced in and out like a tornado answering the call of nature.) My boss began to be sad. She gained weight. The shopping lists she threw on my desk included low-calorie drinks and diet cookies. When her birthday came, she tore up my card and threw it into her wastepaper basket. She filled in flashy lunch dates on her desk calendar. I made her appointments for her, and I knew most of them were fictitious. Sometimes when she came back to the office in the afternoon, she was a couple of martinis over the top. Once, I found her crying over the annual report, though it was even better than usual. No sooner was I accustomed to her depression, which incidentally required me to do quite a bit of her work for her, than she was up again, losing weight, bright-eyed, forgetful, and obviously in love.

One day, I came in to work and found the office empty;

everything had been cleared out. My boss was gone, in due course to be replaced by a younger, prettier woman who made no bones of the fact that her social life came before all the tedious paperwork that I, as her assistant, was perfectly able to do on her behalf.

Not long after my first boss's mysterious disappearance, the store gossip came and perched on the edge of my desk. Though I tried to ignore her so that she would go away, it was like trying to ignore a flamingo or an ostrich that had chosen my little corner of the commercial world to visit.

"You know your old boss," the gossip said, her face glittering with excitement. "Did you know she was caught doing 'it' in the basement?"

" 'It!' In the basement! Good heavens!" I said. I pushed the papers to one side and plunked my elbows on the desk. "Who with?"

The gossip smiled; looked quickly to right, to left. "You'll never guess."

I ran all the store's employees through my mind. Our head of advertising was the only heterosexual male I had noticed in the place.

"Mr. Donato?"

The gossip was disgusted with my lack of imagination. She jumped up, walked away, made a little strutting circle; then settled back on my desk. "Don't be a jerk," she said. "She would have got away with Donato. Anyhow, he wouldn't have done 'it' in the basement, would he? He's got style, hasn't he? She was caught with . . ." she leaned close and I caught a whiff of her perfume.

"Eau de guano," I thought.

"Kowalski!" she said.

"Kowalski?" I repeated dimly.

"Kowalski! Kowalski! Where have you been all your life? Kowalski the maintenance man! Kowalski the janitor!"

I could have cried for my poor old boss, led by her need

to be loved right down to the bowels of the building where, I imagined, humanoids stoked the furnaces. I think it was also at that moment I began to decide to quit the field of commerce and do something more fanciful with my life.

That store still runs at a profit, and so does a magazine I work for which is also staffed almost exclusively by women. They are both headed by unusual females who are not paralyzed about imposing decisions that may be unpopular with their (female) underlings. There is a vast working world parallel to the male's. It is concerned mostly with entertainment, fashion, health and catering. It is run by women, it employs women, and it is supported mostly by women customers. My own first part-time job was behind the counter of a chocolate shop in New York where only one customer in twenty was male, and from that stint among the coconut ting-a-lings of lower Fifth Avenue to the present, I have worked with men sometimes, but always producing for women. Even now, as a free-lance writer, my living and that of a lot of women like me is made from glossy magazines, women's pages, and writing books that I find in shops under "Women's Interest." This distaff ghetto suits me very well, and I'm grateful it is now actually controlled from the top by women as it was not until quite recently. Women in power do employ other women, partly because they would rather not have to pay a man for his services.

The only time I myself have been a boss, the project failed in part because after hiring one rotten apple I could not, even after sleepless nights and endless dithering, bring myself to sack him, thus becoming the agent of his distress and the object of his hatred. My mind shied away from such a horrid duty, as it also did from dreary abstracts of "facing matter," and magazine layouts. All I really wanted to do was write the consoling, solid words, and be on my own to do it. It didn't help that in the midst of transactions with an important advertiser I had to take two days off to have an abortion. The morning I returned to the office, dazed and aching, I found my secretary in tears.

"I didn't want to tell you," she said, "but I've got to tell somebody. I had a miscarriage while you were away."

We fell sobbing into each other's arms. Not only was I unforgivably late for my ten o'clock appointment with the printer, but I had no excuse to give him that he could have understood.

Three or four times I have joined women's projects that were trying to avoid the masculine power structure by doing without any boss at all and submitting every last decision to a committee instead. In my experience, this practice turns out to be all wings and feathers, no brain; and stalemate rules the roost. One day I dropped in at a magazine run in such a way to find the switchboard operator blue-penciling my copy.

"What do you think?" I asked her.

"I don't understand it," she told me, "and if I don't understand it, lots of people won't. It so happens," she said, drawing herself up tall behind her switchboard, "I'm a representative of the lowest common denominator."

Without a daddy, or at least a mummy, to follow and fight, factions flourish (in the cases where I was involved they became militant lesbians against heterosexual moderates), and any individual talent or style must be quashed before it sends up a natural leader, or wit, or financier, who would then by definition be playing the man's power game simply by being better at something, anything, than her colleagues. Of course, it all depends on what women work for—if it is emotional satisfaction, then a loose structure gives everyone a fair share and a good time, even though the product is generally slipshod and always suffers from earnestness, which is the grave of spontaneity.

Whether a man's work is in management, where talking about work is the work, and everything is so abstract—so refined—that lunch becomes worth fifty dollars, or on the shop floor, where the doing of things is done, he has a chance to acquire status in a highly organized system. Colleagues, underlings and superiors are strictly ranked and controlled. The game holds dangers for the plodding worker who does not want to give anyone offense, and equally for the brilliant youngster who streaks to the top by the time he's thirty or so, and then finds nothing in life to be as exciting as his meteoric past. Men are destroyed by drudgery, and equally they are destroyed by hasty promotion. The wounded victors who rose too quickly can be recognized because they are always tooting their own horns, needing to justify to themselves and others how they have done what they cannot really understand, and why they are in positions of power they do not really enjoy. If it is lonely at the top, that's because so many men lose themselves on the way up. Addicted to the game though they are, they've forgotten the point of playing it. When a man is kicked upstairs, to a rung on the ladder above his ambition or unsuitable to his abilities, it is often the prelude to losing his job and falling into that strange twilight business world of boastful men, growing increasingly shabby as the deals they don't quite bring off grow increasingly grandiose.

In preservation of his ego, if not his sanity, a man wants the work he does to be important and carry prestige; to this end men obfuscate, they mystify with jargons, and they create societies composed solely of colleagues; they have trade unions, professional guilds, darts teams and bowling teams, all equipped with rituals and traditions difficult for an outsider to master and particularly unwelcoming to women. In Great Britain, when a medical man attains the rank of consultant, for example, he loses the title "doctor" and reverts to an elegant "mister" as a sign of his increased status. When a British woman doctor becomes a consultant, she is just a "miss" again, and that's not the same thing at all. It puts her in a bag with hospital visitors, medical secretaries, and women no man has fallen for. Professional bodies and customs exist to maintain the status quo, and to preserve male pride in their work. For many men, pride in the job is all that exists as a defense against terminal boredom, and it transcends many other considerations. When I mentioned to my dentist that the man who engineered a renaissance of the Ku Klux Klan in America was one of his profession, the reply was hardly what I expected.

"Fancy that!" he said, "the Grand Gizmo, a dentist! Now what do you think about that?"

"But, Mr. Goldberg, do you know what the Klan stands for?" I asked him.

"Yes, yes, sure. A bunch of no goodniks and fascist bastards I wouldn't give the time of day. But still and all, a dentist! That's very interesting."

Men gather in groups usually according to their jobs, and sooner or later they start to tell stories about great men in their field, whatever the field may be. Male conversation is mostly anecdotal because it is inventing a heroic saga, so if the hero under discussion happens to be, say, a dentist, then the dentist telling the tale, and all other dentists, become a little more heroic. Movies have come out of Hollywood to celebrate cowboys, lumberjacks, doctors, foremen, policemen and such, who lay down their lives for the common good, and at the same time remain incorruptible in the face of temptations as powerful as Raquel Welch. I recently watched a film on television extolling those great heroes, the world's commercial flight controllers. At one moment they were faced with a professional problem of such complexity they were required to call out of retirement the most famous flight controller of them all. I think the actor was the very broad-shouldered Charlton Heston and he said something like "Okay, boys, we have a disaster situation on our hands." He then clamped his jaw over heroic bridgework and kept his cool even, if I recall correctly, while leaping between two airborne cockpits. He succeeded not only in saving Heathrow as we know it, but also in saving his own marriage to a woman who must have been forty years his junior. Flight controllers everywhere were no doubt pleased that their job of work had been chosen to produce a hero of such caliber.

The very same boyish qualities that drive some men to the top of their field make others prefer to go fishing. Not all men are touched by ambition; on the contrary, plenty of them would be delighted to sleep all day in the sun, or be swept out of the pub at closing time, except their wives won't let them do it. Whatever the sex of a man's boss, in reality, he is often working for a woman.

"I support a wife, an ex-wife, three kids, a dog, two cats and a tortoise," an electrician who was "moonlighting" told me. He got out from behind my defunct refrigerator.

"There were some goldfish," he said, accepting a cup of tea gratefully, "but I put a stop to that."

The big winner is a hero among males, even if he is also a ruthless, egotistical son of a bitch: a billionaire, demagogue, or pop idol in whom humility would be a deadly failing because the main reason he keeps on winning is his conviction and faith that nobody else can or should. The big winner is a man for the majority. American presidential elections often pit one of them against a better man, and the winner never fails to win. Every coin in the till has two sides, and clinging to the other side of that one is the admired loser who refuses to play according to the rules, choosing instead to live in open rebellion against time clocks and housekeeping. Weary indifference to common opinion is a gifted layabout's form of "cool," and his brushes with the law, government, work and matrimony give him a patina of melancholy. The seedy hero fancies himself in the style of a private eye, for example, with a bottle of rotgut in the top drawer of his desk, or of a foreign correspondent who files great stories from great distances, as infrequently as possible. Let no tables be booked for the magnificent loser at fashionable restaurants except when high life needs a favor from low life, whose ambassador he is; nevertheless, there is always his seat reserved at the bar of a dive because he did the owner a great favor once. He works for money, but just enough to keep one foot on the pavement. He knows his way around a French menu and the Mozart symphonies, so the world must see he has achieved his condition of divine fecklessness through choice. Women cannot emulate his style because what serves to make a male craggy, raddles a female; however, they certainly find him attractive. God knows he needs reforming! And he needs women too, a lot of them. How else can he continue to defeat the feminine constructs of launderettes, larders, and regular hot meals?

It has been my destiny to know quite a few of these ramshackle irresistibles, and I've seen how they assume the trappings of failure—the debts, the hangovers, the divorces, even a premature death—in their race to be found with integrity and heroic insouciance still waving at the bottom of the conventional heap. They drink a lot. They are also the only men I have ever heard envy aloud the female's ability to bear children, presumably because at points in their downward slide they would have liked to catch hold of a single thing to excuse all the waste. One such darling reprobate has been my friend for more than twenty years, a period in which he has made a few marriages, a precarious living, lots of fans, a few enemies, and a hash of most of his internal organs save only his liver which, oddly enough, is referred to by the medical fraternity as "a monument to injustice." In the way of noble failures, my friend has created a saga of being jilted and of loss, though he himself has done most of the jilting and what he claims to have lost, he threw away.

"I'll always love my fourth wife most of all," he told me once, as he was sliding into his cups.

"What went wrong?"

"She thought I'd change after we married," he said with a wicked smile. "She thought I'd get a steady job. Settle down."

He waved his glass through the fumes of a Soho pub. At the end of the bar a punch-drunk boxer was scrounging drinks from an off-duty Italian waiter; near us, two men were having a conversation in which every second word was "fuck." The former mistress of a crook was asleep in a corner, her head on the table.

"She actually thought," my friend said, "I'd give all this up for love."

8
HOME

Male humans are less complex creatures than females, which isn't to say they are less intelligent; on the contrary, at their best men have vast intelligence, great curiosity, considerable wit, some analytical ability, and even a dash of intuition. However, unless they are describing one of their aberrations such as criminality or homosexuality, they don't spend much time looking for enlightenment in their own sacred entrails, the way women do. Masculine emotions are relatively stable, not subject to hormonal barrages, not victimized by love or lack of love; rather staid, in fact. Therefore, men generally still find it interesting to study, understand, and try to control the world that exists beyond their own experience of it. And a lucky thing for humankind their passionate detachment turns out to be, for it has brought us our greatest discoveries and our most illuminating truths. Self-definition, as women constantly indulge in it, usually precedes rebellion against a prevailing power, and men, sometimes reluctantly and in spite of being numerically a minority, have been the prevailing power in the big world, while women prevail at home. If the modern man should ever be finally prodded into an excess of self-awareness, women may find themselves analyzed into empty houses; for very few men are impressive or at their best in homes that are supposed to be their castles, yet turn out just as often to be their freehold dungeons.

The average man's expectations of a home are minimal: warmth, food, clean shirts, not too many questions asked, and sex when necessary. He has always been willing to pay for these comforts. Ideally a man's work is struggle, and his home is comfort; yet the reverse is often true. At home, he may be threatened by the chaos his life outside is devoted to controlling. In spite of the heaps of status symbols he has acquired to impress other men, he may frequently meet scorn in his own bedroom. The very qualities that make him a success in his work can make him a failure at home, where his decisiveness sounds authoritarian, his inspiration is seen as extravagant caprice, his organization becomes stubbornness, and his scholarship makes the family yawn. It's hardly any wonder so many men have affairs with their secretaries. Office-wives are the most powerful adversaries a home-wife can have because they recognize as their man's best qualities the very characteristics that are deplorable to the wife at home, and they easily forgive foibles that are the last straw in his living room. Three of the happiest second marriages I know are between men and their former secretaries. Because it is the male's nature to retreat from scenes and unruly emotions, he often finds home has become the loneliest place on earth, where he must sit in silence, or glue his mind to television, in order to escape demands that perplex him, and frighten him too by bringing him closer than he has ever been to uncontrolled violence, which is always born of frustration.

In childhood, men are ruled by women who make them eat cabbage and wash behind their ears, who go through their papers, give them a curfew, and demand explanations when they come home late. When little boys are bad, the result is such an almighty scene they soon learn to keep secrets from the chatelaine, or lie to her. Then as husbands, with hardly a free breath between, they become equally accountable to another female who claims her right to know their whereabouts at all times and who, unlike wholesome old mum, also needs to be made love to at intervals, maybe closer or further apart than suit the male libido. Furthermore, she wants cuddles, chaste kisses, and regular tokens of affection that are necessary to her well-being and her untrusting nature. (If she trusted, would she need constant reassurance?) With all the restraints of childhood still imposed upon him by a doting woman, the man of the house is simultaneously expected to be a grown-up: to provide, to cherish like a daddy, to cope with taxes, leaky taps, and things that go bump in the night.

"I'm not your mother!" is a favorite wifely cry, though a mother is precisely what she volunteered to be when they moved in together, and often mother is the only role she knows how to play when she keeps house with a man. He must need a mother, too, or why does he keep getting holes in his socks? For that matter, why does he continue to live with woman after woman if he doesn't need housekeeping?

"Let's play house," a visiting seven-year-old girl said to my son. "I'll be mummy and you must be daddy."

"I don't want to!" my son cried, already on the road to male futility.

It adds to a man's confusion that these days women say they want to be friends and companions who share equal space, and not just housewives. If she really is his friend, then why should she care if he spends Sunday in front of the television set? Or stays out late with the boys? Or goes off for a dirty weekend with a loose woman? Friends don't account to each other for everything or go everywhere together. If friends are wise, they never share a bathroom. Pretty soon, a man discovers that what his friendly, space-sharing mate intends is to complain if he expects her to provide the courtesies his mother used to do. She'll do her share, she tells him, and no more. However, what is her share? Is there no difference except sex between having a flatmate parceling out food and living with a spouse? Who can measure the demands of her work, if she has any, against his? Who can compare their ineptitudes, or their long-range ambitions, or weigh the energy required by them? In the end, home regularly becomes a battleground where two egos slug it out, and where a man finds himself more ineffectual than he has been in any place since the nursery.

Compromise is the magic formula, it is said, for a happy homelife. Yet compromise is hard to define when, say, he wants to live at the south pole, and she wants to be near her mother at the north pole. What does compromise mean then? Presumably, that they live at the equator. Or that one of them "compromises" by living where the other wants to be. Nine compromises out of ten about his homelife are surrenders for the man, and the tenth—his wife's compromise about, say, where he can keep his girlie magazines—can become a source of her unending complaint. Home is a woman's traditional power base, and even now that housekeeping is barely enough to exercise a healthy grown-up's energy, she is generally more at home when she's at home, than he is. Since childhood, in her dreams she has been furnishing her bastion, right down to the weave of the curtains, and the kitchen sink. If she's an old-fashioned woman who doesn't have a job, or who intends to quit as soon as she's pregnant, then as a matter of course she is going to have final say on domestic arrangements while he's cutting and thrusting in the big world. His fantasy of Eric the Red rolling over pine branches with a captive maiden may not quite come off surrounded by the Laura Ashley she has chosen for their bedroom. If there is a room of his house that is his own, a stinking, feral lair where bones of his last kill collect maggots in the corner, the chances are she has had it painted chartreuse.

I once wrote an article for the toughest, most two-fisted, no-nonsense editor in the business. The copy had to be delivered to his home. There, at the end of a short drive guarded by plaster gnomes, I found the rooster had become a capon, small in stature, and daunted before his wife who dusted the coaster whenever I raised my glass. I felt for him and men like him, especially when I was confronted by a furry blue rabbit on the toilet-seat cover. Many men are too shy to assert their taste, or even to know they have any, in their own homes where they are ill-at-ease, defeated, and cowed by chintz.

I went to a dinner at home a few years ago with a California feminist whose husband, a household paradox if ever there was one, stood next to her in the small kitchen cooking his dinner while she cooked hers and mine. They had agreed she would not cook for him, she explained; and he hadn't come round to cooking for her, so they cooked side by side in a righteous clatter of pots and pans. Not long afterward they were divorced. When a man lives with a newfangled woman who doesn't mean ever to have babies and calls him "my friend" while keeping a beady eye on how much he's drinking and where his money is going, he may find it difficult to arrange the practical comforts of homelife. When even the smallest decision must be a matter for discussion, it automatically also becomes a matter for argument, and eventually someone is going to lose. It is often the man who, after numerous small losses, retreats from the carnage that was his home.

Offspring do not necessarily function as a comfort to him in the house, either. On the contrary, babies can blow away the remnants of calm and the vestiges of happy irresponsibility; bills increase, and women, who aren't having an easy time of it either, go off sex for a while, now that they realize what a cataclysm it can effect, and now there is someone else to love. (It's at this point that if it weren't for sexual jealousy, a man could use a second household, until he made a woman pregnant there and it was time to return to the first, where his baby was old enough to call him "daddy" and his wife was pleased to see him again.) When a baby arrives, the man's home moves its center and starts to pivot around the next generation with his wife in service to it. Understandably he can feel like a chosen drone who has made his single flight and has no further purpose in the hive. Even if he helps out in the nursery after his working day, he may be out of place there, uncomfortable, and even guilty because everyone keeps telling him he should love changing diapers and sterilizing bottle after bottle. To make himself and his frustrations effective, he may start to shout as he has never shouted anywhere before; or to pull silence in around him like a shepherd's rugged cloak. Lashing out in confusion and terror at the end of freedom, he has been known to turn into a martinet, desperate to impose a control he does not have. Or he may start staying out late, and coming home drunk to accusations he's bound to get anyway, so why not deserve them?

There are fortunate men who find their homes congenial; not all of them are bachelors; some are contented men who have easygoing wives and well-behaved children who think dad is great. Most men, however, must escape in some way from the homes they have established and support; to this end, they become impassioned fans of something, anything at all, that allows them guiltless hours with other men, shouting, swearing, using foul language, and behaving like heroes on the run, before their dreams are claimed altogether by duty and age. Their means of escape can be innocuous to the point of absurdity: lonely, obscure flights for the bird-men of the marital Alcatraz away from the tyranny of the hearth. They reconstruct the Brooklyn Bridge out of burned matchsticks, tease model ships into bottles, catalogue the ultimate collection of beer mats, compulsively garden, or do other odd things they find totally engrossing and which also require as many hours away from the heart of the family as looking for the Golden Fleece or a new route to the Indies must have done. Women humor tiny manias in their mates and count them a small price for peace of mind; for the fact is, male monomaniacs make faithful husbands and, in my experience, are churchgoers, who often sing in the choir. From time to time, the activities of an obsessional hubby are brought to the attention of a fearless editor with human-interest gaps to fill on his pages. That's why a free-lance woman writer like me has met so many gentle male obsessives, while my boyish colleagues were putting the world to right (or left, depending upon the newspaper's bias). I have learned to recognize a belligerently protective look on the wives' faces that stays there until the women are convinced I'm not going to write anything embarrassing for the neighbors to read. Sometimes, the man's pastime has become a *folie à deux* and a tactic of togetherness with his mate, though this happens only if there are no adolescent sons in the house to give mummy and visitors the message daddy is a kook.

"I ask you, is that anything for a grown man to do?" a twelve-year-old boy asked me while his father was showing off the world's biggest collection of marbles. Even the most bizarre home-based obsessions have a striking innocence about them, perhaps because they are an alternative to something terrible: murder, for instance, or the impulse to put a match under the wife's cretonne curtains.

Many years ago, the editor of an upmarket Sunday paper asked me to interview a couple in Manchester who claimed the wife possessed the smallest waist in Great Britain. I arrived at the terraced house around teatime with a photographer in tow. The door was opened by a cheerful, bearded man in late middle age. Most bearded men have something to conceal, at the very least a failure of jawbone, though once in a while, a man sprouts chin feathers out of an honest superfluity that also brings forth a rumbling voice and a jolly, big tummy like the one that confronted us. Our host showed us into a living room that was crammed with books and half-open filing cabinets spilling folders, newspaper clippings and brochures onto the worn carpet. His wife was waiting for us. She was a busty woman in her mid-forties with dyed black hair, and when she billowed forth to greet us, I saw that her top and bottom halves were perilously connected by a waist no bigger than a healthy man's collar. It was a stunning sight, and frightening too, like being advanced upon by a giant ant.

We sat. We smiled. I put my penetrating questions to her, and she answered in a soft, demure voice, never looking at me as she spoke, only at her husband, who sat in twinkling contemplation of the scene. Gradually, I found myself addressing him instead of his wife. Was her appetite normal? What exercises did she do? Had she always had such a tiny waist?

"Oh, my goodness sakes, no indeed," he said.

"But I don't understand," I said. I was really puzzled. "You told me she never exercises . . ."

"Shall we tell this charming young woman, my own?" he asked his wife.

"Do, treasure," she said in her faint voice.

It turned out that the lady of the house owed her astonishing shape to her husband's fascination with bondage; it extended way beyond fetishism into the country of obsession, and was possessed of a passion more majestic than brute sex. In brief, the man was corset-crazed. Since the first days of their marriage—"twenty years of unrelenting bliss" he called it, and she smiled—he had been lacing his wife into ever-decreasing undergarments until she finally achieved a shape they both found perfection.

"When I walk out with my lady," he said, smiling at his wife who was feeling a little giddy and had folded herself into a cranny of the sofa, "there's not a man in Manchester doesn't envy me!"

Enlivened by innocent joy, he began to pull clippings and brochures out of the filing cabinets and tug books down from the shelves for me to look at. Every piece of literature, a lot of it in French and some in Japanese, concerned the design, manufacture, and adornment of corsets. The material he showed me and the alarmed photographer would certainly have been borderline pornography, except that his absolute confidence we, and all the readers of our paper, must share his delight in straitlacing would not admit a tinge of prurience or anything so vulgar, so common, so downright physical, as lust.

"Do you know what was hateful about Hitler?" he asked, as at last we were making our dazed farewells.

"What was hateful about Hitler?" I asked, feeling very silly, may I say.

"Because of that monstrous dictator all catgut was commandeered for parachutes. And I do mean all catgut. Each and every inch of catgut. I'm talking about violin strings, and I'm talking about corsets. That villain set us back, I can tell you. Things have never been the same since."

"I hope you realize," I told the photographer later, in the car, "we have just seen a happy home."

I used to have a magazine for transvestites in my library. I've often wondered which one of my friends nicked it. There was nothing in that either that could rightly be called pornographic; in fact, it read like a poor man's *Vogue*.

"Shelly uses two layers of Max Factor base to give his skin that healthy glow. Fortunately, Shelly's beard is light. . . ."

As a rule, transvestites do not have a great flair for clothes. A film about transvestism shown not long ago on television featured a group of men notable for the uniform prissiness of their wardrobes, and for the vast number of frocks they had accumulated either at home, with the connivance of a wife, or in rented rooms they kept for clandestine sessions of impersonation.

"This is the only place I feel really at home," one of them said of his alternative apartment.

Their real pleasure, they all reiterated, was not sexual; it came from seeing themselves transformed, and even passing as women in public.

Who is the woman, I wonder, who looks back at a civil servant when he stands before his mirror debating between the puff-sleeved blue nylon and the V-necked red cotton? Here, if nowhere else, a man really needs to have a female "role model." Maybe that's why cross-dressers so often appear to be re-creating the strong-willed and ever-so-genteel mother who taught them what a woman ought to be. When the transvestite is dressing his frightfully proper anima, whom is he disguising? Transvestism, after all, must be at least half a disguise. Isn't he disguising the nasty little boy, with his dirty habits, his loutish drives, and his house-wrecking energy?

"If I look like mama," he must have decided one day, "I'll disarm the old bag, and then maybe she'll leave me alone."

To be welcomed and more or less left alone is what most men require at home; to be accepted as the benevolent boss is nowadays probably, however, asking too much; to be accepted as himself may also be impossible; and in the nest he helped build, to relax is rarely allowed. Whatever the transvestite's sexual appetite (they and their wives swear it is heterosexual), like homosexuals, football fanatics, and drunken wife beaters, they seem to be trying to escape or combat the female's demands and her home rule.

When I was at school I made pin money working for the Gallup poll, putting impertinent questions to the residents of Riverside Drive.

"Am I speaking to the head of the household?" I asked one man.

"My wife's the head of the household," he said. "I'm just the prick who lives here."

9
FOOD

When my father lay demented and dying in a geriatric hospital, I sat at his bedside late one afternoon watching him sleep. It was warm in his room and I should have opened the window, only I was gripped by an overpowering lassitude. My father stirred and opened his eyes. They were cloudy with age and hallucination. He looked at me, surprised to find a stranger in his room.

"Where is the woman who brings me food?" he asked.

My mother had fed him for more than fifty years, right up to the day he died. Long after he could no longer recognize anyone and superimposed phantoms from his memory on us all, she was still bringing him food in plastic pots she took back home, washed, and filled again, cooking from recipes annotated with his criticisms: "not so much salt," "excellent!!!", "use more cloves," "omit pearl onions: heartburn." In the margins of those dog-eared books was a significant chapter of my father's biography, and of my mother's too.

From the nipple to an old man's soup, women provide the common food, and its daily preparation is an act of love that can entrap a human female in a way unique in nature. Cuisine is purdah. Among us, there are even subgroups where families are only happy on a diet that requires the

constant roasting and pounding of fresh spices, ensuring
that the housewife has no time for flirtation, or anything else,
between the midday coriander seeds and dinner's black car-
damoms. If her husband is rich enough to hire cooks, then
he will also need eunuchs to keep the idle females in control.
(In France, clever women have escaped a similar yoke by
encouraging a cookery of such panache it tickles the vanity
of men to take charge of it, at least in public; in private,
Frenchwomen have the processes down to a quick, fine art,
which they supplement with take-away from the world's
most elegant delicatessens and bakeries.)

Food, like sex, is love for a woman and something she
gives in exchange for the coin of her realm that happens
also to be love. The guzzling of female sexuality is in some
ways like gourmandizing—even her sounds of pleasure are
similar in bed or over chocolate cake—and because both sex
and food mean love to her, when there is emotional famine
she treats them as interchangeable. Gluttony has been grandly
renamed bulimia or neurotic binging; however, it remains
predominantly a feminine vice. Compulsive overeating is
endemic to places liberated by Colonel Sanders and his fast-
food pioneers, where women are no longer required to give
love through the metaphor of handmade meals, yet seem
even more desperate to get it that way. Meet a female in
Western society who is grossly overweight, or thinks she
is, and know her emotions are starving for something sweet.

Men tend to be superstitious about their bodily functions,
or why, for example, would they religiously pick their noses
whenever they're stopped in traffic? They think of food as
the sustenance of youth, mama's magic that will rejuvenate
the palate, and with any luck, other parts susceptible to wear
and tear. For many men certain dishes hold a complex,
nostalgic spell alien to women whose consolation foods rarely
require more than a high sugar content. The greatest gour-
met I've ever met confessed to me that his favorite midnight

snack was baked beans, cold, out of the tin; this was the dish he used to share with his father on their fishing trips, and where I could taste only supermarket fodder, he never failed to find the clean, muddy flavor of a Canadian river. I doubt there exists anywhere a graduate of an English public school who doesn't have an occasional secret craving for steamed puddings; and this is true even of those who hated their schooldays, even of those who hated steamed puddings. No man hates tasting the vigor of his youth.

I know a nursery recidivist, an expatriate English antiquarian of distinguished tastes, who disgraced himself during a weekend with me in London on his way back to Rome. I had stocked my kitchen full of fine cheese for him, Fortnum and Mason biscuits, home-made pâtés, and delicacies from Harrod's Food Hall.

"Oh, goody!" he said, upon surveying the contents of my refrigerator. He waved my son's nasty pork sausages and half a packet of bacon at me.

"Let's have a fry-up!"

Despite nostalgia and touches of fantasy, the average male is a conventional eater. Perhaps his timid tastes come from caution. Everyone knows poison is a woman's weapon, and a lot of men have reason to fear their cooks. There is always the risk of a love potion, too, and a man who is desperate to stay footloose prefers not to let a woman make him intimate dinners at home, lest she put something in the food to break his will. Then, too, men doing a hard job of work are afraid a dainty cuisine will sap their strength. It's a version of sympathetic magic. I once helped deliver a racing yacht from Cowes to the Spanish coast, a trip that could have taken more than a fortnight under sail. My job was to cook and to stow our provisions, finicky tasks on a streamlined boat that responds to every breeze like a leaf on a pond. Days of tedium at sea are inevitable, so I decided to make innovative treats to cheer the crew; I mixed a vinaigrette to pep up tinned green beans, and I tucked a few eggs into a box of sawdust where they could survive a gale and emerge as a little surprise after powdered eggs had lost their appeal. With some pride, I showed my list of preparations to the old salt in command.

"Now see here," he said when he had read it, "sling the eggs and foreign muck, my girl. We have salad cream and bully beef on this vessel, or we don't leave port!"

No matter how staid the masculine taste in food, a man's appetite has a gusto that is usually devoid of feminine self-consciousness. The uninhibited way men eat encourages women to mistake food for love (to such a degree that there are women who would no more give a friend a prize recipe than they would give her the man they cook it for). Although there are men who always praise the cook when they have eaten, many of them shovel up what's in front of them, and so what if it's rather special, it all goes to the same place, doesn't it? There are also men who have drunk so much by the time they come to table, they can't work up any appetite at all, can't lift the fork, can't find the right place to put it; can't really pull off eating at all. Sometimes big men, as soon as they feel comfortable with a woman and know her well, eat a lot, fast, and then go right to sleep.

A neighbor told me she knew her marriage was on the rocks when her kitchen became so full of resentment, the food emerged from it sullen and grief-stricken. Women cook their emotions and their personalities into the food. A long time ago, I set out to demonstrate this theory by challenging an American friend of mine to a "ratatouille" confrontation. We agreed to use the identical recipe and the same ingredients in our similar kitchens, and then to compare the final results, which she said would have to be virtually the same, and I said would be altogether different. My friend was an ebullient woman who threw herself onto committees and lobbied for good causes. She lived in a junble of once-beautiful fabrics, clawed by her cats, and interesting objects that had been burned in every available indentation by her cigarettes. She was warm, motherly, and the best friend in adversity I have ever known.

The day of our culinary showdown arrived. My friend brought her "ratatouille" to my relatively tidy flat; it stood on the kitchen table next to the batch I had made. Her dish had first tasting. When she lifted the lid of the pot, the air was immediately redolent with enough garlic to keep a village in Provence for an entire summer. Her vegetables were awash in golden oil, and when she dipped the courgettes out of the pot, they were like fat, green snails floating on the plate. My own restrained rounds were still faintly crisp, in just enough oil to make them glisten. Where was Julia Child in all this? Gone without trace, erased by the personal expression each of us had made of one of her recipes. Fortunately, I could honestly say my friend's "ratatouille" was Wagnerian, bigger than life, really quite wonderful. She thought mine wasn't bad, though she said it would have benefited from a further handful of garlic and another cupful of oil.

Heterosexual male cooks are not excited, they are detached and scientific. Men rarely cook to feed others in the openhanded way women do. Men cook for business, or to show off. There is no question that the most exquisite meals are cooked by men, but then again, the most amusing dinner parties are catered for by jolly women who go just a pinch too far with everything, and who watch, naturally, for reactions to their handiwork yet do not follow each forkful as though it were freighted with ego while saying things like: "Tell me the truth, have you ever tasted a better 'tourte d'agneau à la Languedocienne'?"

Women in commerce and the marketplace suffer from the kind of humorless piety men display when they are lay cooks in the province of the opposite sex. A man I know, like many others of his sex, cooks only on splendid occasions, leaving daily meals to his wife. He is a pleasant, gentle fellow in middle age, an academic who is celebrated among his confrères for being absentminded and kind. One evening, as I was approaching their house for one of his superior dinners, I heard an uproar from within. When his wife came to the door, she was flushed and clearly annoyed. She opened her mouth to speak, but before she could make a sound, her husband thundered, "Shallots!" from behind the kitchen door.

"Damn it!" he cried, "I told the woman to get shallots! Is it so much to ask? A wretched little handful of shallots?"

"Oh, for goodness' sakes," his wife shouted back, "stop making such a fuss! Use spring onions!"

"Spring onions!" he exclaimed in outraged tones. Then, louder, "SPRING ONIONS! Does the woman understand nothing? The recipe requires shallots. 'Use spring onions!' she tells me. 'Use spring onions!' Has she no taste?" His tone became heavily sarcastic. " 'Oh, I'm so sorry, Professor Einstein,' she'd say, 'we're all out of thyme. Wouldn't parsley do, instead?' "

"Who's he talking to in there?" I asked his wife.

"God!" she replied. "He always talks to God when he's cooking."

The male cook's perfectionism is suited to public places where people want to eat as well as they can for the price, and where they don't want their emotions or conversations upstaged by a bad-tempered soup or a "boeuf en croute" that needs its head examined. The male's drive to control works well in the professional kitchen, where he can also indulge his need for systems and status in a hierarchy of chefs and under-chefs that gives no quarter to amateurism. (I have been told that in Denmark a man who masters the intricacies of the smörgåsbord is given the title "Cold Virgin"; if this is not apocryphal, it suggests that Danish cooks are even more controlled than most.) Homosexual males, however, do not cook as other men. My homosexual male friends boast of being better cooks than women, that is the point of the exercise for them; but actually they are only fussier, and more interested in disguising meats than in presenting them honestly. Gay restaurants are numerous in every big Western city. I've been to more than I care to remember with homosexual friends, and even in France they serve overstated, pretentious food, oozing naughty sauces, adrift in promiscuous ladlings of cream, and studded with capers, or green peppercorns, or slices of passion fruit, or whatever is the culinary ornament of the moment. It doesn't enhance flavor or appetite that in most of these fearfully expensive restaurants aggressive lust hangs around like a stinging cloud. These are not eating places, they are cruising places. The air is charged with questing; it reeks of the aquarium in spite of Paco Rabanne aftershave and Turkish tobacco. I often imagine the chef, dowsing cauliflower purée in his libido, dreaming that one of the handsome patrons will be drawn irresistibly by his sauce through the swinging doors into his steamy domain.

There are vast areas on earth where males and females do not eat together, possibly a hangover from the days when hunters were served first with choice bits of the meat they had risked their lives to get; and an atavistic courtesy still respected in the men's clubs of Pall Mall. There are tribes too, where certain foods are eaten by one sex, while they are taboo for the other. When I was a waitress at a big restaurant in New York City, I noticed vestiges of this superstition among modern folk. No woman on her own, for example, ever ordered a gravy dinner, and not once did I serve a man an artichoke.

"Men don't want cold food, like salads and all that, or anything that they think was prepared in advance," a tough waitress, long at the trade, told me. "They wonder what the woman was really doing when she should have been cooking dinner. When a guy orders a whiskey before the meal, he's going to eat beef. Gin drinkers are usually women, and they always order pork. Beef eaters are big tippers and bottom pinchers. Fish eaters are stingy, always worried about their brains or their waist lines, so don't waste time with them. What else should you know? Oh yes, only a real crazy man would order the chef's tuna loaf. You'll find it's big with women." She turned out to be a perceptive sociologist, and correct on every count.

Restaurant tables can be laid as a romantic prelude, always with candles, maybe one rose in a silver vase, music from afar, sometimes no prices on the menu she's given. Food becomes the first tickling touch of foreplay. Men grow stout on meals like these, but stout women are rarely invited to eat them. I had a beautiful, popular flat-mate for a while who used to come home (sometimes) from sexy dinners and race on twinkling shoes to the kitchen where, without bothering to sit down, she bolted cornflakes and top of the milk. She knew perfectly well that if she were to engorge, even on caviar and asparagus tips, or to be seen eating with red-blooded hunger, her admirers would drop her like a hot potato and look for a tastier bit of crumpet with a less aggressive appetite.

10
VICES

Years ago, I lived with my lover and another couple on a twelve-meter yacht called *Dolphin*. She was a magnificent old lady who needed every penny we could spare to stay in the condition her lines and lineage deserved. I was in my mid-twenties, bursting with faith in possibilities and all the ambitious dreams that used to prolong American childhood, sometimes into late middle-age and beyond. With a few other friends, we four had sailed *Dolphin* through the Bay of Biscay from England to Gibraltar. In retrospect it was a dangerous venture for inexperienced mariners like us, though at the time it seemed a perfectly understandable, even sensible, thing to do. By the time we tacked into Cannes on the French Riviera we had shed members of our crew at various ports and were left alone with literally not a bean in the galley. At the start, we tried to charter *Dolphin* until we learned that rich residents in that part of the world kept their own boats, and holidaymakers preferred engine to sail. We ate stale loaves and drank cheap wine, downing our spartan crumbs with jokes, laughing all the time; until finally, even the bread ran out. I answered an advertisement in a local paper for a teacher of English to the sulky children of a local family, while my lover, who was older than the rest of us and a glamorous South American, charmed his way into a job behind a hotel

140

bar where he mixed pink ladies and flirted with sunburned tourists.

"You two are the pillars of our community," the skipper used to say when we came back from our onshore jobs and pooled our earnings to buy groceries. The skipper himself had read Anglo-Saxon at Harvard and neither he nor his wife, a former schoolmate of mine, had anything at all to sell, so they stayed aboard, keeping *Dolphin* shipshape and practicing to be the poet and the painter each was going to become as soon as the time was right.

Just as it was beginning to seem we were bound to spend the rest of our lives attached to survival by a gangway, we had a stroke of luck.

"It's a godsend! Once in a lifetime," said the skipper, training his binoculars on the American fleet that had sailed in overnight and was tied up outside the bay.

Our skipper, it happened, was an excellent poker player. He always scooped up the matchsticks we used to stake in games that we played on deck, with the lights of pleasures we couldn't afford a few yards away; and he had played for real money too, during his National Service. In the face of fiery disapproval from his wife (she had never needed to have a job, and did not grasp the relationship of money to freedom) we decided on the spot to open a floating poker school.

It was easy to put the word around, and in no time at all we had our suckers. The four men arrived one at a time after sundown and slipped on board quietly in the dark. Different players gathered most nights. Introductions were whispered by moonlight before they crept below to gather around a table we had hastily covered with green baize. There was no reason at all for the hush-hush—we were hardly a threat to the local casino—but the suckers liked it, and so did we. We even took to shipping the gangway before the game began.

"We're beyond all laws here, except the laws of chance,"

the skipper often said, and it always impressed everyone.

When the players were seated, I collected from each of them only a little more than I had spent on drinks and cold cuts. It was the skipper's winnings we were really counting on for our profits.

"It's childish make-believe. It will come to no good. You're all ridiculous," the skipper's wife grumbled, including me in her complaint because she could see I was enjoying my role as a shady lady of the smoke-filled den. Certainly, I preferred it to explaining English prepositions to brats who watched me with malevolent, scornful eyes.

"At-up-in-out-by! *Quelle sale langue!*" one of my pupils had cried as he threw his textbook over the parapet of the balcony into the sea.

The skipper's wife started going to bed in the forward bunk as soon as the game began, making enough noise to demonstrate her disapproval. My lover never returned to the boat from his job before midnight, and the men were playing in the salon where he and I slept, so I usually spent most of the night outside, alone, going down every hour or so to serve food and freshen drinks. Skylights were set into the deck in such a way that by moving from one to another I could see the hands being dealt below, and observe how the men played. At first, I watched because there was nothing else to look at except the stars and shore lights. Soon, however, the game began to interest me so much I fancied putting a pearl-handled revolver in my stocking top and trying my luck at the table.

"No dice," the skipper said.

It was late, and we were arranging his winnings into neat piles.

"This is a serious enterprise, and women can't play."

His smugness was all the more annoying because I saw his point. I had noticed in penny ante games of my past that men played systems, tenuously attached to logic, and women would play hunches. Although neither was infallible by a long shot, the male's methods required arithmetic, at least, while the female's needed no more than luck which, as everyone knows, is personified by a fickle "lady." Women are easily distracted from the game too, their concentration routinely broken by conversation and street noises. A psychologist I know calls it the female's "atavistic ear," ever tuned to a cry from the nursery; whatever value this may be in the homestead, it's no good at all for poker. Furthermore, I had no money of my own, and to borrow a stake from the skipper's winnings would have been unfair. Deep down I knew I would not be able to bluff a confident man (just knowing that, meant I couldn't do it), for if I succeeded, he'd never forgive me.

From my vantage point I saw that as soon as any normal male seats himself at the gaming table, hey presto! he becomes a cowboy, a loner, a white hunter, a free agent, a cat who wouldn't flap in a typhoon, a cynic who knows the score, no stranger to violence, a cool bastard who was tattooed in Yokohama; he's a tough guy, baby, his scruples are no higher than his holster, and when his pale eyes meet yours, look away. Plump American sailors, with wives at home saving for three-piece suites, flick cigar ash, swill beer, and narrow their eyes over a pair of pasteboard fives. Gangly youths glare at each other across the table.

"You son of a bitch," one says to another, as he pats a phantom dagger on his belt.

Emotion is utterly controlled, while chips and money shift their weight around the table, and the boys skim along on their voyage at the edge of vice.

"Two whores," says a freckled redhead, whose mother probably buys his underwear.

The skipper's mouth twitches around a cigarette, his steady hand turns a card, his smile is snake-thin, and his physical resemblance to Groucho Marx, which has given us endless delight during the day, looks as little comforting by lamp-light as a jokey mask on an armed raider.

In the long run, beyond luck and even beyond skill, the man who wins is the one whose heroic cool persuades the others they have to lose to him, and this means he must first be persuaded of it himself. Bluff is the thing, and bluff begins at home. Weakness is really tested in a winner. He is a rare bird, and in our skipper we had him. On the few occasions he met his match, I scurried from skylight to skylight to see lesser players fall away as the two masters fought with the concentration and minimal exertion of true expertise.

Though I can't pinpoint just when things began to change on *Dolphin*, change they did. The skipper's deadly poker air started to intrude on our daytime life. No more hilarious swimming off *Dolphin*'s side because he needed to sleep nearly all day, and he shouted at us even when we tiptoed on deck. He stopped doing Groucho Marx imitations, and sat by himself in a coil of rope reading William Burroughs and smoking. Sometimes when I spoke to him, perhaps only to ask what he'd like to eat (his wife spent her days in silence on an air mattress in the sun, so cooking had fallen to me) he seemed to summon his spirit back from a distant place.

"Three eggs, easy over. Two slices of bacon, crisp. Fried potatoes," he'd say. He had taken to eating a perpetual breakfast, and he never added "please" or "thank you," either.

He had stopped being any fun at all.

"If you knew the truth about him," his wife said to me once, "you wouldn't be so pleased with him. Or yourself," she added, contemptuously.

Finally, after a month, my lover and I told the skipper we thought it was time to move on to Antibes.

"You go," he said. "The boat stays here with us."

When I looked at his wife for an ally, she lifted a copy of the *Herald Tribune* in front of her face, and said nothing.

Up on deck, my lover and I whispered about leaving *Dolphin* as soon as we had enough money of our own, and he agreed to stop putting all his earnings to the common good now that the poker winnings were sufficient. We would go back to Paris, maybe even find proper jobs. Whispering, afraid to be overheard, we felt treacherous and trapped. Something had begun to trouble me, something vague and niggling; I couldn't tell if it was the season, or the beginning of a bad cold. I was in love, of course, that was a familiar feeling, and it wasn't that. I knew I wasn't pregnant. One afternoon, I went alone to shop in the market with all the French housewives; their children stood behind them carrying loaves bigger than themselves. The good, kitchen smells were everywhere. In front of me was a small hill of perfect oranges and one of them was solid in my hand, when suddenly I was faint with panic.

That night, still worried, I watched the game from above. The skipper was directly in my view. I saw his two jacks and a six on the table. He had lost weight and he was smoking constantly. I'd have to go down soon and empty the ashtray at his elbow. Only the man across from the skipper, and directly under my skylight, was left in the game. He'd been a canny player; his chips were stacked neatly in front of him, like a miniature skyline. A king, a four, and an ace were showing on the table, and I had seen another ace, his down-card, a "bullet" that could make mincemeat of the skipper.

"Down and dirty," said the dealer, a skinny boy who had been consistently outclassed.

He flicked the last cards. I looked down as the skipper's opponent bent back a corner of his new card, just a little, barely enough for him, and me, to see it was a third ace. Judging from the cards dealt around the table, I knew there was not the least possibility he could lose. He never twitched, and he increased his bet, not lavishly as I probably would have done in my excitement, just precisely enough to confuse the skipper, who shifted slightly in his chair and raised his head so that suddenly his eyes were straight on mine. There was the smallest twitch of his eyebrow, and I knew he wanted me to signal his opponent's hidden card. Nothing could have been easier. The skipper and I had been friends for years; it would have been enough for me to do no more than think the words, and he would have known the score. In that instant, I recognized the most dangerous male vice: the skipper had lost the courage to lose. The game had taken over, and his ego was fighting without honor or shame for its life.

I backed away quickly before I became an accomplice in his downfall, and maybe in my own too. Several deep breaths of salty air put my head straight. I looked up and saw a full moon riding at the top of the mast, like a target in a shooting gallery.

Years later, after we had all gone our own ways, the skipper's wife turned up at my London flat; she was newly divorced, and angry.

"Tell me something," I said late in the evening, "do you remember the time you said, 'If you knew the truth about him'; what did you mean?"

"You thought he was saving our bacon, didn't you? More fool you," she said. "He had just inherited a small fortune. He could have bailed us all out anytime he'd wanted to. He was hooked on the game."

A decade after that, I heard from a mutual acquaintance that the skipper had gone through his inheritance and had become addicted to heroin along the line. He was traveling all over the world, surviving on poker wins and minor drug deals. I've never known a junkie's soul to stay alive for long; heroin addiction kills it. I've lost more than one friend to that poison. Nevertheless, I am persuaded no man is destroyed by games who has not already been mortally wounded by life.

As men see it, vice is never in the game, it is in the player, and weakness is the only vice. All the deadly male vices are derived from imitations of heroism, which are as necessary to a man's well-being as intimations of love are to a woman's. To refuse the challenge of dangerous encounters with drugs, say, gambling and especially ubiquitous drinking is thought unacceptable cowardice, precisely because the risks are high.

"I never trust a man who doesn't drink," says one alcoholic man friend of mine whose doctor has warned him any glass now will be his last.

When a man pits himself against a potential vice it isn't only a test of his strength and his "cool," it is also one of the last life-and-death struggles remaining to him in our society, and one he undertakes at first with jolly companions; then later, he goes alone. In the beginning it's all very romantic. However, if he loses his contest, he will be so cruelly driven he will need to resort over and over again to the game that has dwindled to no more than a momentary killer of the pain it, itself, creates. Junkies do not love junk, gamblers hate the cards, alcoholics are made sick by drink, and whoremongers long to be chaste. They are trapped first by a weakness pleasure has discovered, and then by self-disgust, which is eased only while in the very throes of compounding itself.

"Drugs," a clever man told me, "are what men take them for."

Laws against potential vice actually create new vices, and even technological progress raises mischievous challenges. (I've often wondered, for example, what heavy breathers did for kicks before the telephone was invented.) Now that the planet is no longer a great adventure playground for men, wherever the smallest chance exists to test himself, to do something risky, even something dastardly, some man will try to get away with it. When the swimmer isn't as strong as he imagined he was, or the current is as treacherous as the flow of heroin through a needle, then the sucker is in trouble. He can be trapped in the relentless spiral of addiction. He can die. A commonsensical woman expects her sons and lovers to stay out of the water rather than test themselves in it, and if she can, she orders them to, or tries to deprive them of the means for their dangerous contests. I used to know a woman who on the day of a major horse race unplugged the telephones, hid them, and put every stitch of her husband's clothing in the trunk of the car, which she then drove to her mother's house. She deprived him of money—it was all hers anyway—and left him on bread and water for most of the season. Somehow, he still managed to lose the shirt he didn't have. Unfortunately, to take away the means by which men sink or swim does not remove the weakness from men. There were as many alcoholics during Prohibition in America as ever; it was just that some of them didn't drink. Others, instead of being drinkers, became illicit drinkers, and many drank because it was illicit.

Being the most powerful animal on earth isn't much fun or profit for a man if his strength is never tested. Some men accept an intellectual challenge and rely on the muscle of their brains. A considerable number of men, who are too afraid of losing to try, succumb to the vice of laziness, yawning behind a fist and complaining nothing is quite to their standards, so why bother? Other men see their daily work as a contest; if they go too far, they sacrifice everything real to the abstracts of money and success. Men can work in an efficient team and most of them prefer to work that way because it assures status among companions. When that worthy impulse is frustrated, however, in men who are young and vigorous, they feel their egos growing flabby without any exercise, and they go ape. They form renegade gangs to mug senior citizens. They rip the seats out of railway trains. They challenge other gangs to crazy warfare no sane male would dream of undertaking on his own, or see any reason to at all if he weren't drawn along with a tide of others.

During the Algerian war, when I lived in Paris, I was walking home one night from a friend's house. Gradually I became aware of a sound that swelled moment by moment until it flooded the small back streets, and I felt myself teetering over a mindless, angry ocean. Although I never even saw the riot, which was reported next morning in the papers, the very sound of it, stitched with machine-gun fire, put wings on my heels. Anything that roared with such abandon was not going to be susceptible to argument or charm. I'd be very surprised if anywhere on earth there exists such explosive power as that generated by a mob of excited men. A man's intoxication with it could make him a war hero or it could make him a hooligan, depending upon the circumstances.

What is triumphant mateyness in the members of a team of athletes becomes fear of losing face among rioting fans. What is control to a platoon of well-drilled soldiers facing an enemy becomes depraved pride when warring boys meet on an empty lot of the inner city. Furthermore, put bulls on motorcycles, give them studded leather jackets to wear, and assign them places in a column of hoodlums, and there will always be some little cows delighted to ride pillion. The most perverted heroes attract camp followers who compete in their own ways for pride of place. Someday their progeny, if they live to have any, will be the settlers who colonize new planets; however, for the moment they have nothing to do except destroy this one.

To need a loose woman is one of the oldest professions of heroic maleness. The prettiest was a reward to the bravest.

Even now, in countries where there is no disgrace attached, almost every adult male who can afford it will have his innings with a pro. In our communities, however, the female requires her male to find it in her, and her alone, his only woman, and in her he must find all women, presumably including a whore. Women's magazines are not embarrassed to advise their readers regularly on erotic techniques of stunning lubricity. A recent book called *The Complete Guide to Sexual Fulfilment* by Dr. Philip Cauthery and Dr. Andrew Stanway, written for a lay readership, as it were, has an explicit illustration that shows a man opening a car door for a woman who is not wearing anything at all under her skirt. The caption reads: "By deliberately or 'accidentally' exposing herself this woman is certainly making his life more erotic. Incidentally it'll also ensure that he will open the car door for her in the future. . . ."

The authors do not say whether the man opening the car door for the provocative woman is a minicab driver, a passing stranger, or her lover, even though what could incite the first two to rape would merely make her lover's life "more erotic." It is my impression a lot of men really don't want their lives to be "made more erotic," thank you very much; they would prefer a cosy fuck from time to time and a good night's sleep. With wives and girlfriends suddenly posessed of techniques no whore could afford to employ, competing with a man's fantasies, and sometimes with the man himself, for preeminence in bed, the male is threatened by failure. Given a choice between a panting tigress and a docile pussycat, I daresay the average man would rather live with the kitty.

It humiliates a man to admit he goes with prostitutes because it means he can't seduce a nice girl into doing for love what a professional does for money; however, frequently all a man's dreams contain is no more perverse than acquiescent, undemanding sex with not an apron string attached to it, and this, of course, is the single thrill no woman can give for love. (Though there are rumors of women who give themselves for love of sex, nymphomania is like the dodo: it lives mostly by hearsay and doesn't sound a very pretty animal.)

Men usually resort to whores and brothels for ease rather than excitement, for comfort, not delirium. Even if a man gets off on menace, he doesn't want an unexpected demand or a surprise from store-bought sex. On the contrary, he wants exactly what he bargained for, and that does not include anything that could result in his failure; he gets enough of that at home. The scene he enacts with a prostitute, no matter how bizarre, is one he has planned down to the color of her garters. He is in control. Maybe he even designs a scenario too bizarre to spring on an amateur in order to justify going with a whore. Whoring is a profession of lethargy or despair. It requires nothing much from a woman, no imagination and minimal theatrical ability, just a little universal equipment. Laziness in a whore is a real virtue. When men say, as some do, all women are whores, it's Mantalk for all women are lazy; and vice versa. One English tart tried to persuade me she was doing a service to the community by acting as a kind of overflow pipe on the social edifice. If whoring can be seen as a service, then it is a passive one that exists to be used and forgotten. A whore is a hotel room for a tired male ego.

It's unusual to meet a man among us who will confess he has been with a prostitute for some sexual rigmarole unless there is a funny story attached, and it happened in another country. I've heard several times, for instance, about gorgeous Egyptian harlots who revealed themselves behind the tinkling curtains of their cribs to be males in drag. And what about the Parisian "filles" so impressed with milord's virility or charm they give themselves for free? They abound in the folklore of Mantalk.

I knew a few French tarts in Paris, and, I'm bound to say, they were the meanest, most grasping and pragmatic females on earth.

"All men are shit," one of them who lived in my hotel used to snarl whenever we passed on the stairs.

"Tell me," I asked her when my French was good enough, "why do you always say all men are shit?"

"It's very simple," she said. "They stink."

Suckers pay for an illusion of carefree infallibility. However, everyone, including the whore herself, now sees the deal as contemptible, and therefore the sucker can become so sunk in contempt the only energy he can summon at all comes from more contempt, until he finds, as some men do, he can no longer get it up at all unless he pays for the privilege. I remember a prostitute who told me she thought it was charitable to chain willing men to table legs and feed them from dog's dishes because that was what the darlings wanted, didn't they? Like everyone I've ever met who boasts of charity, she had grown fat on contempt. Any human being so overcome by terror of his sexual passion he needs a chain, a boot, and a curse to permit himself to feel it, is serviced by the contempt of his mistress because it reinforces what he feels about himself, and what a lot of women, not all of them whores, still feel about male sexuality: that it is beastly, blunt and contemptible.

For the most part, men try to keep their vices in brothels, casinos and racetracks, or at home. Alcoholism, however, overflows all boundaries set upon it, and alcoholics are everywhere boring companions over and over again with whatever reminiscences remain in their diminishing gray cells. Partly because of my profession, and mostly because I don't object to "just the one" myself, I know a lot of heavy-drinking men and women, and it seems to me the sexes don't tipple the same way. Women rarely see their vices as contests—more often as deliberate paths to oblivion. Because they want to be swept away, they put up a smaller resistance than men do; thus, when they go too far they are more entirely doomed. When a man is a drunk, for instance, wallowing in his maleish fear of failure, he'll still find no shortage of women who want to reform him and love him. He can go on gathering love even if he can't do much with it in the sack. When a woman is a drunk, however, she is utterly claimed by her primary fear, for she becomes unlovable. An unlovable woman is an embarrassment to her society because she shows up its lack of compassion and the animal nature of its sexual dealings. A man can "take advantage of" a drunken woman, whereas a lot of women break their hearts over drunken men. The ability to suffer over a drunk is in itself a feminine weakness that is practically a vice.

It's my own feeling that women turn more often to food than they do to anything else for their idiosyncratic addiction. Gluttony is mostly a female's vice, as sexual insatiability is mostly a homosexual's vice, and the two are not unlike each other. Both disorders are deafening overstatements of "I want," and both suggest an inability to achieve satisfaction. Why eat twenty eclairs if one is sweet enough? These aren't appetites, they are deranged hungers. I used to have a flatmate who could eat a large jar of peanut butter, a half-pound of butter and most of a loaf of bread at a sitting. Sometimes she made herself sick afterward, but once I came home early and found her at table with a bucket into which she was spitting the food she had chewed. In every other way, she was a bright, fastidious girl, yet when her vice claimed her, she lost all control; and then when remorse followed, she had no recourse except once again to her vice. I know homosexual men who go to specific pubs and clubs where they have it off in the men's room with strangers before taking home one or two other strangers they pick up as casually as I do my telephone. The greedy and the promiscuous want, want, and want, something they are apparently not getting, or why would they want it so badly? And if they imagine they are not getting it because for them it cannot be, that makes them want it all the more. At the end of a long love affair, when a woman wants to have back again dreams that are gone forever, she too can become wildly promiscuous for a time. (She also, incidentally, loses or gains weight.) The period of my own life when I was tastelessly promiscuous, and painfully thin, began in misery and ended finally when self-disgust was mitigated by hope, and I knew I no longer needed what I couldn't have, and I would do as well, even better, without him.

The male bulimic (or "glutton" as such used to be called before feelings were so easily hurt) is a relatively rare creature. Men prefer competitive vices. To drink companions under the table is one thing; to eat them under it lacks dignity. I daresay all men would be driven to insatiable sexual poking too if their physiology allowed it. Even though a heterosexual male can have six or seven different encounters in a week, and manage two women in a day if he is desperately trying to keep one a secret from the other, he won't be able to keep it up for long, and it is he and he alone who has to keep it up.

Untested ignorance is pretty in children and here and there it is still considered an asset in marriageable women. A teetotalling male virgin over the age of twenty or so, however, unless he has been called to the priesthood, is not an object of respect. On the contrary, he's more likely to be a figure of fun both to his own sex and the other one. Personally, I see the point. To be ignorant and good is a dinky virtue compared to being wiser after a fall.

11

SPIRIT, RELIGION, AND HUMOR

If there is only one God, those who believe in Him are quite sure He's male, just as Mother Nature is female. The way we feel about God and Nature reflects the way we feel about the two sexes. God is never wrong, not even in a temper. Nature, on the other hand, is illogical and unfair. If God invented Nature it was to test mankind, and if He invented mankind it was an expression of divine, supernal, and altogether masculine ego: that they should glorify His name. However, if Nature invented us she did it entirely by accident and pays us no more heed than she does fleas and trees and other by-products of her brainless passage. God is stern. Nature is stubborn. For the most part it has been given to men to celebrate God, who is honorable, while women satisfy Nature, who is lunatic. As soon as we came up with one God, men became His priests and women, naturally, became witches.

Any man who longs for holiness and purity of mind and body is going to have a lot of trouble with women, or at least a lot of trouble with himself when women are around. His spontaneous susceptibility to the image makes it very hard for him to pray when his flesh is rising, willy-nilly, in response to the curves of a passing girl; and cautionary tales full of ironical wit have been written about his failure to do so. A devout man can only make sense of the conflict between spirit and body if, whatever he says, he sees the female as representing misrule, ungodliness, and temptations of the devil himself. Through her, nature works an evil distraction, and the woman has to conspire at it out of her own weakness. Any man devoted to an order from God that includes celibacy is bound to view women with something like horror until he subdues his lust (why else has God given it to him?) and is able to see women with pity and condescension, as the elect always see unfortunate others who are doomed to live in an absence of grace.

Where men must be holy, a "good" woman is one who makes herself as inaccessible and unattractive to them as possible. Ideally, she goes into purdah, or becomes self-effacing and demure; or better yet, constantly pregnant. Even then, in the eyes of God-fearing men she isn't free from animal necessity. The cloistered nun, for instance, must menstruate like any slut in answer to a pagan, lunar summons which she has no intellectual power to subdue or control. In a hostile land, the purest female can increase the danger to a heathen male soul by enticing him to rape which, as it is a fate worse than death for her, must be a crime worse than murder for him. Among orthodox Jews and some other faiths only boys can be confirmed. The rites and dogma are taught exclusively to males because femaleness has always been regarded as a primeval, ineluctable vocation which is impervious to instruction. It's this impression of the female as a minion of Nature's brute function and as a base, dangerously glamorous necessity that makes men object to women in the priesthood, where a spiritual and intellectual rigor is supposed to be required beyond any witless call of nature, and even in spite of it. A celibate priesthood cannot ever permit women to enter its ranks because, as they see it, a female cannot ever exorcise the devil from her flesh, or prevent herself from causing the pollution and wickedness of men. This, at least, is how a young Greek Orthodox priest explained the situation to me, with grave courtesy, when forbidding me to look closer at some icons in an area of his church closed to females of any species.

Some minority ecstatic faiths let women rant from the pulpit; however, most priesthoods that accept women tend to be pastoral and to see their duty in modern terms as being primarily toward their fellowmen, not the ancient, uncompromising, ritualistic celebration of God by those made in His image. The modern pastor consorts increasingly with social workers and less often with angels. No doubt many horrified clergymen, particularly those who live in esoteric splendor, judge this to be a triumph of female housekeeping over the male's divine inspiration.

In traveling, I've noticed that in those poor countries where hardworking wives have the least reason to respect their own husbands, many of them show a feeling for their celibate priests that resembles romantic love. This can pose a great sexual threat to a young priest and force him to keep a wide distance in every sense between himself and the very members of his flock most eager to adore him, and possibly even God through him. If he dared show simple, humane tenderness to one troubled woman, how could he be sure the love-starved creature wouldn't attach herself to him, and then might all his hard-won purity not go to the devil?

I was invited to an "encounter weekend" once in the 1960s, when it was fashionable to meet for sessions of letting it all "hang out." In the therapeutic group was a handsome young priest who raged about the agony of his unchastened flesh when women in his congregation came too close. A pretty girl sitting next to him wept with him and then, when he had finished his anguished tirade, she threw her arms around him to comfort him. His face was a mask of torment; hers, I thought, of naughtiness. The celibacy of a handsome man is no sign of God's love for women.

To be full of spirit and inhabited by a distinctly male presence has a different significance for a woman than it does for a man.

"Go ahead and convert me," I told a young missionary in training. "I'm fair game for you."

"I can only tell you that Christ entered into me!" she said, her face radiant. "He made me happy, and he can do the same for you."

Organized religions strike me as being men's societies devoted to exalted ritual, while the women's auxiliary branches take care of creature comforts. I once spent a week in a convent writing an article for a magazine. Most of every day I worked in the kitchen with giggling novices whose bustling good humor even during the hours of enforced silence was charming, as was their industry. I was touched by the sisters' discretion when over my bed I noticed a faded outline on the wall where apparently the crucifix had been (though whether they had removed it for my sake or for its own I could not know). Even though the services I attended were lilting, they lacked the sonorous majesty of men's voices raised in a Roman church, or the plaintive timbre of the cantor's tenor, and they compared to the men's services as a breeze to the wind. (I must confess I like rituals to be sensational, and I don't think I could believe in a God who didn't feel the same way.) Women love well and can devote their lives to the most exacting service with humility and joy; moreover, some women achieve a pitch of revelation. Nevertheless, there is an intellectual access to worship that, with notable exceptions, seems open only to the male.

A pious misogyny is found among high-church clergy and also among some intellectuals and philosophers whose contempt for women is not without a gingerish tinge. The monkish dismissal of all but a few females from these rarefied circles is frequently accompanied by a tendency to collect young male disciples and, sometimes, to extol platonic male relationships, or even a more explicit version of brotherly love. When a great artist comes out of this echelon he generally hightails it to the South of France or the Austrian Alps as fast as he can. Most of the men who thrive in intellectual shelters are critics of other men's work or are peculiarly cryptic, tight-assed poets. Gay spirits in timid bodies of high intellect are found at every university and, I daresay, have been since universities began.

When I was at Columbia University in the 1950s, some of us from the women's college, as long as we promised to behave ourselves, were permitted to "audit" lectures at the men's colleges. I once attended a class being given there by one of our leading scholars on the Greek plays. The great professor stood at his podium and looked down upon our faces, raised and eager for knowledge.

"There is a female in this room," he said. "She will do me the courtesy of leaving it."

I left. He was not a man for argument. Once, when he had been bullied or bribed into delivering a lecture at my women's college, he chose to speak for an hour in what purported to be ancient Greek. Oddly enough, I remember it as being one of the most enchanting lectures of my university career. The morning was balmy in mid-May and the big windows of the lecture hall were open on to the gardens. A sparrow blundered in on a breeze and flew round and round, as confused as any other soul there, until finally it found its way out again. Meanwhile, the professor never broke stride, his strange words circling too, out of our reach yet, somehow, tickling the edge of consciousness.

Systems and hierarchies concerning man's soul are the most severe of all his disciplines, and the most laden with rite and ritual. A soul is invisible, mysterious, wonderful, and must pose a great challenge to men bent on control. Wherever men make a system for soul-saving, they make a lot of trouble for themselves and everybody else, because such a system is forever being threatened by other systems, as well as by anathema and skepticism. Males have all through history been called into battle on behalf of their soul-saving systems, either with the promise of glory in the hereafter (sometimes including some very earthly pleasures indeed) or in the conviction they are fighting the forces of evil down here. I suspect more men have died saving soul-saving systems than saving souls. The male spirit craves an enemy and worthy opponents, and what could be better than the devil himself? (An opposing football team will do at a pinch.) How is a man to be sure he's right in his faith, commitment, and patriotism unless other men are patently wrong? Although women are contentious too, they are much more practical and attached to the facts of existence. They are less keen than men to die en masse for their beliefs though they will kick up a fuss for the vote, for the safety of their children, for (or against) free abortion, and for other improvements on their own patch.

The spirit is a general and amorphous kind of thing, and speaking generally its great gift to men is imagination. Its gift to women is intuition. Intuition is a matter of knowing something faster than knowing how it is known, and it's a very useful talent on a dark street in a big city, say, or when face to face with a liar, or when in a position to help someone who is too troubled, shy, or ill to explain what he needs. It's valuable too in intellectual pursuits where it analyzes clues that may be overlooked by a mind in the throes of invention. Imagination, on the other hand, leaps forward from understanding to understanding to something that has not been seen or understood before. It's imagination that makes men—though not a lot of them—great artists, and intuition that makes some women wise. It is also intuition, and not tender, maternal, "caring" feelings, that makes women excellent doctors and in some countries has given them that profession virtually for their own, as it may do in most of the world some day. Because they analyze backward from what they know, to find out how they know it, talented women write good "whodunnits." They have also created a special genre of sensitive, sensible "women's novels" that frequently concern themselves with autopsies of dead love; rather like Harlequin in reverse. Very rarely, however, does a woman create a world that is at bottom not the common one, or write words that lift off the page to unknown places and describe creatures who are not, or who are not yet. Even more rarely does a woman show the genius that puts sounds together into an order of music bearing witness to an almighty spiritual power, while actually creating it. Of course, society's reluctance to waste education on women (and the reluctance of women themselves to be educated and thus become less attractive to the run of men) has handicapped them in the arts as in all other ways; nevertheless, there have been great women artists, certainly enough of them to make anyone think about why there has been no transcendent one.

A sense of humor is a sturdy companion to the human spirit. Isn't it a crying shame so few men have one? Humorous men are so rare that a homely, short, bald, pauper who can make women laugh will have all the gratitude fucks he can handle. On the other side, however, a woman who makes funnier jokes than a man won't last long with him, which is one reason women keep their senses of humor among themselves. Granted, comedy must be a nerve-wracking calling for a male, keeping him nose to nose with his own overriding fear of failure. Most male jokes are based on impotence, inferiority and bungling; and most male jokers embody humiliation or attack a straight man who embodies it, or compel an audience to laugh at its own humiliation. There are plenty of male comics who raise a laugh by their way of saying the words of other men, and there could never in history have been more men who rouse hilarity simply by making a face; however, we are very short of those comic geniuses who are in possession of an ironical truth and don't take themselves seriously.

Privately men engage in sessions of competitive joke telling at which women are not welcome. Laughter at these impromptu contests is a gauge not of wit, rather of gratitude for a familiar performance. Simply the common preface "Have you heard the one about . . . ?" means most of the joker's audience have indeed heard it; however, they will laugh anyway as a measure of his performance against the last one. All men's jokes are practical. They give the teller a group's attention for a moment or two, and they are rarely inspired by anything more than ego. In Mantalk, it is often said women have no sense of humor; in translation this means women do not laugh at jokes they have heard before or at jokes that aren't funny, unless they are in love with the man who is telling them. Moreover, women know men find their laughter ambiguous: when a woman laughs, how can a man be sure she isn't laughing at him, instead of his joke?

A woman who has been around understands that men would far rather laugh at her than at her jokes. The woman who cannot tell a joke, is a joke. Nevertheless, I have always found women to be funnier in private than any men in public, possibly because a lot of jokes are a form of complaint, and women have complaining down to an art. An inspired woman uses her own words, not somebody else's, to laugh at herself and to laugh at what her sex takes most seriously: love. Women gifted for humor do not rehearse their stories; they make them up as they go along. It isn't a theatrical performance, but a private donation of encapsulated experience.

"What do you say to those men who keep asking if they're the best you've ever had?" a girl asked a group of older women once.

"What I always say is, 'Yes, darling, I'm afraid you are,' " one of the women replied, " 'but I live in hope.' "

Men who will roar with laughter when another man drops his trousers on stage call women's wit "bitchy"; certainly, it bites, and it doesn't wag its tail. However, to do a classic "turn" for an audience of men still requires a sacrifice of allure most women find as difficult as a man would, say, to show his audience he really does have the smallest penis in Christendom, instead of hinting at it from behind a zipped fly.

Late one night last year I was walking in the East End of London with a group of friends, one of whom is a respected architect, when we found ourselves outside a Hawksmoor church.

"Stop," said the architect. "Look. This is possibly the most beautiful building in England."

Without a word of jargon, he then explained to us the craft and subtlety of what we were looking at. He wasn't teaching, he was sharing what he knew about the building and its architect, and he was doing it with love and humility. I've known painters to talk with similar faith about paintings. Come to that, I have a friend who lights up from inside when he tries, hopelessly, to make me adore computers. I find these men very attractive and truly in touch with their spirits, no matter how silly they are about sexual love. It is when I'm listening to them, my intuition tells me that the male's soul is a department of his brain.

12
FRIENDSHIP

If sexual desire and friendship had not turned out to be mutually exclusive, I would possibly have liked a lot of the men with whom I have been in love; however, lust engenders a definite hostility, no doubt to justify the aggressive aspects of coupling. Making love is just not friendly; in fact, friends avoid doing it except perhaps for consolation when nothing more titillating is around and, of course, when they have burned through passion together and are fortunate enough to discover themselves married to people they like. Ideally, we would marry old friends, and go to bed with new ones.

Men and women don't even meet with an eye to friendship. If they're young, they meet for mating and if they're mated, they meet for hanky-panky. Even a husband who is allowed out for a night with the boys won't get time off to see a girlfriend, or a former girlfriend. The very word "girlfriend" is usually a euphemism for doxy, mistress, paramour, as a "boyfriend" is for a lover. As for married women, it is more difficult for them to have men as friends than as lovers. If a wife is so much as seen alone in a restaurant or shopping in the supermarket (especially shopping in the supermarket) with any man other than her husband, everyone is going to assume they are having an affair, or he is a homosexual; possibly both. (They probably are having an affair, or he is a homosexual; possibly both.) Not long ago, I was taken to lunch by a group of leisured California women, who were married to middle-class doctors.

"Do you know what, girls?" said one of the older wives. "I've just realized I haven't been to lunch alone with any man but my husband in twenty years."

"I know exactly what you mean," a younger wife said. "I've never been unfaithful either."

Even in their dotage and decrepitude, there is lascivious surmise on both sides when the sexes meet; it's irrepressible, it's cute, it's natural, and it's about as friendly as a war between giant squids.

It doesn't advance intersexual friendships that each sex has a different notion of what the other means by a friend. Friendship for men is a condition of expansion: the more the merrier. For women it is often a matter of contraction: two against the world. Male friendships want to be out and doing things together; in contrast, to go out for a woman almost always means to go out with a man, or for a man, or to put herself in a position to be approached by men who are out for a woman. Men have clusters of friends, while few women are happy without a "best friend." "My best friend" is a phrase with a feminine sound to it (as is "my former best friend"). Female "best friends" talk every day in person or on the phone; they consult on the smallest decisions, and they know each other's every movement.

"Where were you?" I've had best friends of my own ask me accusingly. "I've been trying to get through to you all morning."

Best friends exchange insights as casually as they do their clothes, and they complain about outsiders, especially men and lesser friends, as cheerfully as they might about the weather. If a best friend is not working or if she has no children, she can become as jealous of a third female breaking into her friendship as she would be of one breaking into her marriage. I've known women who stand in the position of best friend to several others and who do not like to introduce their best friends to each other, even trying to keep them apart as long as possible, because they know that in these tight circles everyone talks about everyone else, and to be absent is to be dissected mercilessly. What else are friends for? If any pair of men were as exclusive as two women best friends, they would be marked as homosexuals; women, however, are seen with a more Victorian eye by society, and their friendships are generally considered innocent which, it happens, they usually are in a sexual sense, though emotionally they can be so demanding and require such claustrophobic fidelity that if it were possible for a man to become a woman's best friend, he'd find the difference between friendship and a love affair is not much more than a fuck.

By feminine reckoning, men don't have friends at all; they merely have mates. Women see this as a failure of masculine sensitivity, though it could as well be seen as a triumph of action over reaction, and deeds over opinions. When men meet it is generally to do something together and then, later, to talk about what they have done. Women meet specifically to talk; sometimes they talk about men, though not so often as men suppose, and not nearly so often as they talk about each other and themselves. In fact, women can become friends with nothing more in common than opinions, particularly about each other and themselves. Although this makes for intimacy, it also means as soon as one of them changes her mind, or outgrows an opinion, or is bored by it, the friendship founders, and worse, because women hug their opinions close to their hearts, the friendship ends in hatred. Nobody hates like a former female friend except a former best friend; come to that, nobody is more hateful. Confidences are betrayed, lesser friends are parceled out just as friends are when a couple divorce, envy breaks surface, and no occasion to do emotional or psychic injury is overlooked, particularly when the women concerned are proud of the refinement of their feelings.

Women give their friendship as they do a vote, as a mark of approval, and since nothing is more to be approved than approval of oneself, they are susceptible to flattery, which is why, for instance, pretty girls often have plain friends. Women's friendships are volatile because like a vote, approval can be changed, it can be withheld, it can be lost.

There were two music students in the girls' dormitory where I spent my first college years. One of them was beautiful and she played the piano with flamboyance that glossed over her errors as well as, sometimes, the composer's intention. The other was a plodder and incessant player of scales. The plain girl worshiped the pretty girl, and so did the pretty girl; this was the shared opinion at the heart of their friendship.

"Listen to the darling!" the beauty said to me once as we stood in the dormitory hall that was always redolent of powder, chocolate and sweat. "She's trying to make music. Bless her!"

Although I thought the scales sounded crisp as raindrops, I was no musician, so I smiled agreement.

At the end of our second year, a recital was organized in the common room and everyone turned out for it, including a celebrated professor from the Juilliard School of Music, which was attached to our university. The beauty, tossing her mane of auburn hair, played some auburn-hair-tossing music; and then the plodder played Debussy études with so much elegance and blissful simplicity, even the great professor stood up to applaud.

"That little bitch, my former 'best friend,' " the beauty said a few days later when we met in the elevator. "I taught her everything she knows. All she did was take, take, take!"

When a man elects a special friend, he does it because they have shared an adventure together, or he offers his friendship as payment for a debt incurred. The ultimate debt is for one man to owe the other his life, and this is one of the heroic romances. If "best friend" is a female invention, then "blood brother" is the masculine reply. "Blood brothers" are a pair of heroes who have been blooded together in an initiation ideally involving shared danger and violence; they may not meet for years at a time, yet each knows the other will race to his side if he needs help and even die for him should it be necessary, which, in the common run of things, it never is.

"He's a man I'd choose to have next to me in the trenches," a schoolmaster said to me once of his "blood brother," another schoolmaster, even though the most dangerous thing either of them ever did was confront sixth-form boys with irregular French verbs.

The work, games, sports and vices a man undertakes in his imitation of heroism are the fields where he makes his buddies and hopes to find a "blood brother" with whom he has a mystical bond he cannot explain to his wife, who is likely either to loathe her husband's "blood brother," or to seduce him. (Or both.)

It's true that opposites attract. That does not mean, however, that they like each other. The fact is, lusty, heterosexual men are not usually comfortable with women. They mistrust feminine sexuality, detest the weakness of their own flesh and fantasy before even the silliest woman, and do not like women at all. On their feminine side, a lot of women resent the uncomfortable, self-abasing things men make them do to be attractive, resent their need to be attractive to men, resent men, and do not like the brutes one little bit, all the less if they cannot live without a man of their very own.

"Just like a woman!" men say in scorn.

"Male chauvinist pig!" women say in anger.

If the word "Jew" or "black" were substituted for gender, the Anti-Defamation League or the NAACP would prick up its ears (and if "gay" were, all hell would break loose); however, crude prejudice is allowed between the sexes. Women who complain most bitterly when the slur is against them continue to be bigoted and haughty in the way they talk about men.

Male homosexuals do not cease to be men; between them and women there can exist a relationship that is edgy, though useful, sometimes containing a little mystical quality of blood brotherhood, as well as the fickle intensity of best friendship. There are very few declared homosexuals who do not keep some females around as passports into the world of feminine glamour, and surrogates in the beds of heterosexual men. The gay man, in his turn, is a valuable escort for a sophisticated woman who is without a conventional male; he is tolerant and unshockable, and also liberal with comforting cuddles which a woman doesn't expect from other women and rarely gets from heterosexual men. He is her poppet, he is her pet, and he is dangerous only if she falls in love with him, or goes to bed with him and expects him to change. As far as a woman is concerned, the ambivalence in her charming companion is not that he fancies men (she probably does too), it is that he does not fancy women.

For a woman to become a homosexual's moll she must be inordinately afraid of lusty males or, more likely, heterosexual males must be in mortal terror of her. Fag hags are frequently women of dash, celebrity, or unconventional abilities, who threaten the heterosexual male's ego because he fears he will be impotent with them; and so they turn to homosexuals for male company despite the sexual rejection implicit in the relationship, or even because of it. Like most of the cleverest women, a fag hag is frequently distinctly masochistic in her dealings with men, having learned to relish pain as an attention, at least, from those too afraid of failing to offer happiness. Even though a fag hag is also often a great neurotic or alcoholic, if her fame and glamour are enough, her homosexual friends will continue to adore her and, toward the end, one of them may even marry her to become her servant and her heir, long after former heterosexual suitors see her only as a raddled, imperious old bore. The ideal fag hag is worshiped by men, yet is beyond any man's love, promiscuous, yet inaccessible and lonely. She is the sort of doomed goddess a homosexual male wouldn't mind seeing in his own mirror.

I would probably have lived like most females, aware of the sweet nature of my hairdresser and tolerant of his aftershave, except that early on I had an encounter with a man who was for a while my dearest friend. During a long, hot summer in New York I took a temporary job, the way many other university students used to do, in a big department store. Gradually I became aware of a man at the counter next to mine who was ostensibly selling ties, but who managed to spend most of his time reading paperback books, which he stuffed hastily into his pocket whenever his internal alarm warned him a supervisor was approaching. Even after all these years I can close my eyes and see his small, delicate ears. The first thing I noticed about him were his ears, and I continue to remember them, though I can't recall the color of his eyes. They were narrow eyes, amused and knowing. His eyes made the permanent sales staff bitter about having to tolerate a young man who was so clearly moving on to better things, and they made the customers embarrassed not to be shopping at a better store. Because he was older than I, and aloof, and a male, we didn't meet very often; however, I used to watch him walking to the subway after work, always alone, at a swift, irregular pace, feet turned out and knees slightly bent, as if some eccentric secret called his tune. Anyone who knew America in the 1950s will understand why it was decided among the staff-room gossips that he was probably a communist. It was easy to see he had a subversive intelligence, and in those days of national paranoia it was generally assumed the only aberrations were anti-American. Much later I learned that even though most intellectual homosexuals are attracted to left-wing policies, their fantasies are Pharaonic and their deepest inclinations are fascist.

Out of boredom, I imagine, he began to talk to me, mostly about the books he was reading. These were volumes of poetry and history that I used to buy and read as fast as I could in order to have something to share with him. We started going out for a drink together most evenings after work, and sometimes on Saturdays we went to films. All around him, practically warming his dainty ears, was a growling aura of sexuality. I was a virgin at that time, and his musk allured and repelled me freakishly. Eventually, of course, I fell madly in love with him. I cannot recapture now the feeling of loving him so wildly I couldn't sleep and nearly starved the female out of my body. It isn't necessary for me to feel as I did then in order to remember and believe that I loved him as much as I have ever loved any man.

Hundreds of us loved him. At the bars he took me to for drinks there was a club of men and women, boys and girls, and me, bound by our passion for him. We used to meet sometimes just to talk about him. He was a monster. He loped among us with his penis always in half-erection, bulging, as if he kept a vegetable to ripen in his pocket. Although he said he'd lost count of the people with whom he had been to bed, he rarely went to bed with those who worshiped him, only occasionally with women, and never with me. He pursued dark, Latin types mostly who were not interested in the books he read, or anything else for that matter except their profiles between two looking glasses. He had graduated from a university in New England with high honors and was supporting himself temporarily by selling, or failing to sell, ties. I put to the back of my mind the thought of summer's end when he was going to take up his graduate studies at a midwestern university and I to start at Columbia University in New York, so we would probably never see each other again.

To my way of thinking, his intellectual triumphs made his sexual preferences even more perverse. I was not surprised or offended that he preferred going to bed with men, only that he chose to go to bed with fools. He fucked across the board, but he was enchanted by vacuous boys and scoundrels.

"It's hardly worth rejecting women," I grumbled once after a swarthy pickup had run off with his cuff links, "if that's the best you can do."

"Let the punishment fit the crime," he replied.

Only years later, after I'd had some troubles of my own, did I realize he must have meant that both the crime and the punishment were his.

Because of him, I learned about the homosexual underworld in New York at the time. He was my entrée into cellars where men danced naked, and my introduction to young junkies with painted toenails and glittering eyes. After he left for university, there was no place for me to go for solace or company except back to those basements in perpetual twilight where the barmen knew me by name and there was always someone ready to weep over a hopeless love. Even for a heterosexual female, gatherings of homosexual males held a dizzying sexual possibility. Pretty young men flirted with me, and though I knew they did it in order to appear virile to the real objects of their desire, for me to be flirted with at all was enchanting. And they were witty! The irreverence of those catamites and buggers made me laugh. It was in New York, where I never achieved a social life of my own, that I became a bona fide fag hag out of loneliness and love of a homosexual: two perfectly compatible conditions.

My circle of homosexual men friends gave me laughter, music, and places to go. Most nights there came a time around midnight when I sensed a metamorphosis was about to take place and if I didn't hurry home to hide my head under the pillow, I'd have to watch footmen turn into mice and coaches into pumpkins. Sometimes I stayed too long and saw strange sights; usually, however, I left before the magic ran out. Perhaps because I had loved the first homosexual in my life, the excessive behavior of my friends did not shock me in the least, less even than the squalid heterosexual deals of a generation that saw the wedding ring as a prize for being very good, or very bad.

Years later, I used to meet some of my former homosexual cronies when chance brought us together. By that time, I was a practiced heterosexual with a group of my own friends. I was no longer mad about the boys, but I felt an attachment to the old frenzy, a responsibility almost, and it kept me by them even as many of them entered a peevish middle age that made me often the butt of their drunken abuse and, even worse, of their hungover remorse. Just as the two conventional sexes need role models, so do homosexuals. I have known many of them to fashion themselves into latterday Oscar Wildes, unfortunately without sharing the master's original gift for self-knowledge.

Fag haggery and motherhood do not combine easily. I wonder if my homosexual men friends would have forgiven me a daughter? Few of them forgave me for having a son. Though I know some heterosexual men who seem to enjoy playing with babies, my homosexual men friends, after suggesting I call the boy "Xerxes" or "Caspar" and put him down for a good school, lost all interest in my household. One of them would not visit me again after the time my baby distracted me from conversation. He stormed out of my house saying there wasn't room in it for two Hitlers. Years ago, in the throes of a liberal convulsion, I hired a young homosexual to be my *au pair*; it was a disastrous experiment, for though the boy doted on me, he treated my baby son with evident distaste and jealousy, thus making it impossible for us to be friends.

I recognize an element of superstition in the way homosexuals see me and other women. My infant son and I once shared a holiday villa with a dear old friend whom I had not seen in many years. On the return trip, he got amazingly drunk.

"If this plane were to go down," he said in a spitting rage, "you'd save the brat instead of me!"

He was correct. In the unlikely circumstance of choice, I would have saved the child. Given a choice, I would have saved the child even if, as all the air hostesses assumed, it had been his child. Probably that was precisely why he had never wanted a child of his own and took the extreme contraceptive measure of being homosexual. But why had he imagined it would be in my power to save anyone's life? He, and others I have known like him, see all women, and fag hags most of all, as untrustworthy magicians, sly witches with supernatural powers, born to sacrifice. "Sprung of Circe's Isle," my first homosexual friend wrote on the flyleaf of a book he gave me. At the time I thought it was the prettiest compliment I would ever receive and, dazzled, I missed the threat.

Despite the anomalies that must arise in a relationship with males who both covet and despise her sexuality, a fag hag has fun with her boys. If she has a heterosexual sex life, her homosexuals thrill to talk about it with her in the most intimate physical detail. A fag hag is never closer to her homosexual male friends than when they join in furtive, giggling mockery of heterosexual males, as servants do of their employers, or children of their teachers. I've been told homosexuals are close to each other in mockery of women; however, they have not been discourteous or brave enough to do this overtly in front of me. My own impression is that most homosexual males are fearful of women even to the point of sexual repulsion, and also fascinated by them. Whatever their innermost feelings about each other, homosexual men and heterosexual women can be playmates in a way that becomes impossible between normal men and women once they are much over the age of five. Homosexual women, on the other hand, though they often have platonic heterosexual friends of their own sex, are very rarely relaxed or happy around heterosexual men whom they regard with the utmost suspicion and fear; probably that's why they are homosexual women. In the scheme of friendships it seems that the heterosexual male, due to the role and position for which nature has designed him and like any other boss, is most often left out in the cold.

13
OLD MEN

Time is not a cosmetic. Nevertheless, a man in his fifties and beyond can remain attractive to younger women, particularly if he has accumulated money, prestige, power, and the very same marks of experience that ruin female allure while making a man craggy. Even though women can become more interesting with age, the interest is not sexual. Seasoned men do not generally want a challenging mate. They prefer physical companionship, a degree of tacit obedience from a helpmeet, and a pretty, public hint of their continued prowess in private. Men can even go on helping to create babies into old age, if they shed spouses along the way. Nature does not prolong the female's fecundity to the same degree as her mate's potency, and this is merciful; the processes of reproduction require an exhausting donation from women that merits early retirement. In spite of the male's reprieve from sexual scorn, the day must come in his life when prostate or prostration belies the lore in Mantalk about century-old Georgian peasants stiffened by vodka, and all his great mystique can no longer disguise his decrepitude. In short, he will no longer be able to get his great "it" up.

Sexual purpose, which is as good as saying "sex drive," lives inside a female all her youthful existence; some women

176

call it a consolation, others call it the curse. Even when age puts her beyond childbearing and makes her less moist and welcoming, she can still make love out of nostalgia, or affection, or habit, or fear of loneliness and lovelessness. The passive nature of sex for a woman means she can continue to receive it, to give herself, and to think herself a victim too, after fucking has ceased to be strictly necessary. When age unsexes a man, it does a more thorough job. It castrates him. For good or ill, castration softens his beard, blunts his thrust, changes his bite to a nibble, makes him generally physically weaker, and feminizes him. How a man responds to time's gelding probably depends upon how he has felt about life, and about sex. The impotence of a monk is no cause for regret. On the contrary, he may want to celebrate his honorable discharge from an area of lifelong self-control. I daresay Don Juan would join him happily in a bachelor's retreat, equally relieved of an existence spent in flight from the triumph of women. The man for whom sex was a temperate delight can probably surrender it easily at its natural conclusion as a pleasure plumbed. It is frustrated desires that cause anguish in their passing. Aging in dignity for either sex demands that appetites should be relinquished at the moment they are being taken away; the only way anyone can live in concert with nature is to do what she is doing to him. This is a delicate transaction: some men hang on desperately beyond performance and others who have been confused by sex, or humiliated, or bored, opt out too soon and throw it away before it's quite used up in order to acquire the illusion of wisdom that is reckoned to accompany celibacy.

"If there's one thing I've learned . . ." say these premature graybeards, and the phrase is usually followed by bad advice such as "Never give a sucker an even break," or "Never drink red wine with fish," or "Never trust a woman," or similar evidence of the absence of time's only real gift to either sex, which ought to be a sense of humor.

Many old men sit in the sun stroking a cat or a grandchild, engrossed for perhaps the first time in their lives by slow, feminine sensuousness and enjoying it. However, there are always codgers who rebel against the retreat of virility and who continue to try to get a leg over long after they haven't a leg to stand on. Infirm lechery is a male dementia similar to the one that makes some desperate old women prance around in sequins. When the sex act has been only an allegory of power for a man, he is bound to grow old in cantankerous denial of impotence and to treat women with contempt, blaming them for what he is no longer able to do to them.

Pointless lust is found especially among old fellows whose lives have been devoted extraordinarily to control. For control-mad men sex must always have a prurient and voyeuristic overtone; it is something to defend themselves against, something to inflict on women. I've been told about a revered statesman who in his senescence asked his secretaries to work naked, ostensibly so he could prove how he had at last overcome his flesh, and how unmoved he was by their beauty, even though his moving parts had long before seized up. I suspect most of his pleasure even in youth had come from looking, and from looking at himself, looking. Women will do daft things out of respect, if not out of love, and apparently he found girls ready and thrilled to be admired while helping him prove his strength of character. Any male, even an ancient shadow, who requires service will always find women to serve him.

"He's been spoiled by women all his life," a friend said in apology after her aged father had groped my left breast.

The feminine confusion of sex and love is widely put about as a new morality. Although this helps excuse the sexual fusses we get into, it does no favor to the aged, many of whom have reached a time when they would rather the fucking stopped. People cannot be persuaded to do what they are incapable of doing; nevertheless, a lot of men and women don't trust themselves to know what they want to do, and are predisposed to think themselves wrong. Thus, they will heed the "experts" even in areas where there can be no expertise beyond personal experience and imagination. How many of them, quite content to settle into well-earned celibacy, have been persuaded by articles and books on geriatric coupling to extend their sex lives beyond measure, as if the bare motions of fucking, long after prowess and need had departed, remained a magical ritual to inspire love?

"As a man gets older he needs increasing amounts of excitement and stimulation to obtain and sustain an erection," wrote Doctors Cauthery and Stanway in *The Complete Guide to Sexual Fulfilment*. "All can be well if he has an understanding and willing wife who is able and prepared to stimulate him more as the years go by. However, many women, especially in the older age group, are so inhibited . . . they cannot bring themselves to do what is necessary."

If "all" is not well and the husband's tumescence cannot be achieved, let alone assuaged, by his hardworking wife, presumably he's justified in trying it on with the checkout girl from the supermarket, or his secretary, or his daughter's friends. The failure is not his, it's his wife's, and the suggestion is that she doesn't love him enough, because when sex is love, should one fail, so does the other. Necessity is the mother of invention, but invention cannot create a real necessity, only an unnecessary hunger. If an old man and his mate enjoy continued sex, that's fine; but if it starts to be hard work for both of them, perhaps it's time they tried to enjoy something else together.

Because men are superstitious about matters of the flesh, a flagging male is ready to imagine youth will enliven him again if he possesses it in the shape of a warm, young woman. Once upon a time, when I was in my early forties, I went out to dinner with a man who was over seventy, well-traveled, amusing, and I assumed growing old in philosophical dignity. (I should have known better. I'd read the autobiographies of aged philosophers.) I thought he was interested in me for my mind. The lunge he made in the front seat of his car was without prelude or invitation. Pinioned as I was, our encounter could have concluded in rape, or in its geriatric equivalent, for the fact is he had no erection, but I physically fought my way free. In spite of the rebuff, he rang me again, and he happened to mention he had recently divorced his third wife because she was a "gold digger." He said she was thirty-eight.

"Is that so?" I said. "Four years younger than I am."

My septuagenarian hung up as fast as he could, and never bothered me again.

"He says you're a nice person," a mutual acquaintance told me later, "but he's only interested in girls under forty."

It's generally said age is cruel to women, depriving them of juice and beauty; however, age is much more cruel to men. Because a woman's life is marked by physical surrenders to nature, she is prepared for a gentle twilight. There can be great happiness for a woman in old age; there can be authority, time for herself, and freedom such as she has never known before: freedom from being available. Men, in the meantime, have seen the passing years as rungs on a ladder always upward, moving toward goals. Sexual and social impotence take them by surprise and embarrass them. When they retire from active life, they age rapidly, even tragically. Time pushes them out of the only world they ever had time to know into a roost ruled utterly by females. The life of extreme old age centers around food, elimination, mild exercise, body heat, and other concerns at which wives, mothers and nurses are adept whether the object is a baby or a querulous old man. When an old woman has her old man, no matter what kind of rake, philanderer, or tyrant he was in youth, she has him by the balls. He is impotent and can no longer offend with infidelities, he is delicate and can no longer frighten with his recklessness; if he remains excessive or bad tempered, he is likelier to kill himself than to murder her. All he can do is complain, and like as not his complaints make her feel needed by him, maybe for the first time in their lives together.

Among women, the delusion of illness is often a lifelong condition, guaranteeing the attention of family and doctors and, particularly when in the form of headache or lower backache, excusing them from sexual activity. In healthy men, hypochondriasis strikes later, which is to be expected in physiques that have suffered no more than bruising by outside agents and are beginning to feel for the first time twinges of mortality that are familiar to even the healthiest woman for most of her life. Anything that escapes a man's will, he sees with resentment. Time is out of his control and so is its natural erosion of his physical powers and stamina. When he starts to complain of every ache and hiccough, he is in fact complaining of his mortality. He wants a cure for clocks and calendars. My father, for example, called old age "diabetes," which he never had, and "cancer," though there was not a sign of it outside his own imagination, and a dozen other pathological conditions I found annotated and underlined in the *Merck Manual of Diagnosis and Therapy*, his favorite bedside reading for at least twenty years before he died in his eighties of old age. The male's ego, useful to him in his youth, does not allow him to accept the universality of natural processes when they dare to happen to him.

"Growing old," my father used to complain, "is murder."

Age is comeuppance for the strong, proud male animal. Too often his only recourse apart from complaint is boasting, which men always undertake in proportion to their sense of failure. Boasting is the first aid to an uncertain ego peculiar to the male, heard even in the playground, and it is often also his last, when time has carried him past his prime to a flat, dull country run by women. In any society that comes up with longevity, enforced retirement, and small family units featuring monogamy, not much will be as humiliating as an old man's dotage. His wife rules the little queendom he gave her, his children criticize him, his grandchildren are noisy, his doctors condescend, his appetites, hairline, and sex organ have receded, his cronies are dead, dying, or locked into boxes with their own wives, and nobody listens to the word that wanted to be law. There are social and physical reasons why men die on average before women; it could also be some of them prefer to.

When my father was into his seventies and my mother about a decade younger, they went to live in a place my mother calls "Geriatric Gulch": a tree-lined new town in the eastern United States where old people who can afford it live in elected isolation. At first sight the community is like any other tidy American suburb; only gradually are small differences apparent that account for the impression a visitor has of being on foreign soil. To be an outsider there is like landing in an outpost of the old commonwealth, where familiar customs and language have been subtly adjusted to suit Methuselah. Curbs slope, and electric sockets are all at waist height to spare old backs; it is possible to lead life without climbing stairs, and even the smallest cottage has two big bathrooms at its center, fitted with gleaming prosthetic devices. Carpets are high-piled over layers of foam rubber, all appliances are run on electricity so there is no need for matches, or flames, or anything deadly to the absentminded. Temperatures in every room can be controlled by a touch of the finger on a dial calibrated for failing vision. A hospital unit is set in discreet shrubbery near the clubhouse. Armed guards at the gates protect residents from muggers, radicals, door-to-door salesmen, and children. The minimum age for joining the community is a relatively youthful forty-eight to accommodate second, third, and even fourth wives of old men. Should one of these lasses fall pregnant I daresay a bylaw requires her to pack up and leave. Children are subject to strict apartheid and watched with more caution than affection. Even grandchildren are allowed to stay only for limited periods and to splash in the olympic-size pool for precisely two hours every morning, not one instant after the guard has blown his whistle and shouted "Kiddies out!"

"What harm would it do to let them swim a little longer?" I asked an old woman one August day when the thermometer was touching one hundred.

She wrinkled her wrinkles. "They 'you know' in the water," she said.

Cleanliness is a fetish among the aged middle class, and incontinence becomes a sensitive issue in a community where many of the residents are beginning their second childhoods. Sex remains an issue too, of sorts. Mildly pornographic magazines are on sale next to knitting patterns in the community shop and my mother swears there is a local prostitute, herself no chicken, who services some of the old men with "aural sex."

"The men talk," my irreverent parent says of this transaction, "and she listens."

Contrary to society's conscience, which abhors a ghetto, this odd community is safe and cheerful and seems to offer a genuine solution to the pain of loneliness among the aged of both sexes. There is even history and folklore growing up around the place. The last time I visited, for example, everyone was buzzing about a little old spinster who had been accosted by a little old man on her way back from a class in origami at the clubhouse.

"Hello, beautiful," he said, "I've been watching you."

The woman, who was a bit hard of hearing, smiled cautiously and looked puzzled.

"I say I've been noticing you!" roared the little old man. "I'd like to roll around in your sheets and eat crackers in bed with you."

The spinster ran all the way home where, quite breathless, she rang the main governing body of the community, the Entertainment and Recreation Committee, to report the incident.

"What happened?" I asked the gleeful octogenarian who was telling me the story.

"Oh, they caught him right away," she said. "He apologized most profusely. It seems his vision isn't what it was, and he mistook her for a young girl."

The place is jumping with spry, chirpy widows, and a new widower doesn't last long. No sooner has his wife passed on to life's reward than he is inundated with invitations to intimate low-cholesterol dinners. Usually, he succumbs within months to one of the blue-rinsed predators and the union lasts happily, "ever after" being a relative term. Occasionally, however, the widower goes away for a while to some southern resort and returns in a Hawaiian shirt with a forty-eight-year-old hoyden on his arm, to the dismay of the community and, no doubt, of his heirs. Mother insists the December end of these marriages rarely stays upright for long.

When my parents had not been long in their peculiar community, my father and I took a walk one morning so that I could have a look around. The houses were brand-new versions of traditional eastern American architecture. They were named for battles in the Revolutionary War. They all had mock chimneys in which, mother said, mock birds made their nests. It was one of the sharp autumn days special to the country of my childhood. Days like that put

me in mind of the September apples my brother and I used
to pick from our father's trees. When we bit into them, they
sizzled, and the sweet white flesh became increasingly tart
toward the core, so we shivered as we finished them, and
our mouths were puckered as if we'd been sucking lemons.
I was thinking I would never taste an apple like that again,
and my father sighed as if he'd had the same thought. We
stopped for a moment under a maple tree that was blazing
in its last gasp. Leaves were dropping already; they lay like
embers on the pavement. I put one in the buttonhole of my
father's jacket. He had become quite a dandy in old age, but
I noticed with a little shock that he and I were the same
height, though he had been a tall man and I had years earlier
stopped growing.

"It's very nice here, dear," I said.

His mouth was turned down at the corners in crotchety
disapproval that made him look like a disappointed child.

"I don't like it," he said. "There's something queer about
this place."

Two old ladies in track suits and headscarves jogged gently
past us.

"Good morning!" they trilled.

My father turned to watch them with disapproval as they
bounced into the distance.

"You see what I'm getting at? Whenever I go for a walk
here everyone says 'Good morning.' "

My father was a born New Yorker. He had been held
up once at gunpoint, and never again looked a stranger in
the eye.

"That is not natural," he said. He shook his head. "What
do they mean by it? I don't even know these people."

"Don't be silly, dad. They're not muggers."

"Respect," he said, mournfully, with none of the old
anguish.

We walked on. Golf carts were swarming toward the

manicured links that lay in the center of the community. Every season four or five players gave up the ghost right there, summoned in the midst of battle to their final hole-in-one. Mother told me the Entertainment and Recreation Committee had tried to disguise the ambulance as a golf-cart so it wouldn't alarm the residents. In the end that proved too difficult so instead they painted it to look like a Bloomingdale's delivery van. I told my father this story.

"Your mother will never grow up," he said, and sighed again.

Two old ladies in fur jackets pedaled past on outsize tricycles.

"Good morning!" they said.

My father grunted. A flock of Canada geese flew overhead in V-formation and we watched them until they were no bigger than nail scissors on the horizon. The next year on a similar fine day in that same place I was to see them flying again, hear their funny, sad honking cry, and mourn for the old man.

"Life is good," my father said.

He put his hand on my arm. It looked like a little, bare branch.

"This place is not for me. I don't like it here. Haven't you noticed something about this place?"

He tried to smile in the way a man does when he is afraid he's about to be scorned for his feelings.

"Look around you," he said.

I looked around. Ahead of us an old woman was walking briskly toward the community shopping center. Four Cadillacs passed in convoy; each was being driven slowly, ceremoniously, by a white-haired granny sitting bolt upright behind the wheel. On a bench near us three old dears sat perfectly still, smiling at the sun. They looked like three little egg-shaped Russian dolls carved in wood.

"Keep looking," my father said.

Across the road a woman dressed like an African explorer
in khaki and a pith helmet was cutting asters in her garden.
Closer to us, practically underfoot, a fearless rabbit nibbled
late clover. Rabbits were a great problem there and, according to my mother, kindhearted old ladies tiptoed out
at dawn to leave them carrots laced with contraceptive pills.

"Do you remember when you used to shoot the rabbits
in our garden?" I asked my father.

He made a dismissive gesture.

"Just keep looking. Can't you see? Don't you notice
anything?"

There was nothing left to see that I could see. Somewhere
someone was playing a record of Lena Horne singing
"Someday he'll come along, the man I love. . . ." The sound
was so faint that if I hadn't already known the words, I
wouldn't have been able to make them out. A little old lady
popped out of a side turning. She was swinging a cane as
if it were a scythe.

"Morning!" she said, striding on toward the church.

"Aha!" my father said to me. "See what I mean?"

It wasn't like him to be so mysterious. My father's nature
wasn't quizzing or playful. On the contrary, he took most
things with more seriousness than they deserved. He had
forbidden my brother and me to play gin rummy when we
were children, lest we become gamblers.

"See what, dad?"

"Women!" he said.

Women. He was a virtuoso with that word. He could do
anything with it. He could drag it up from his raging heart
or send it through his nostrils like tobacco smoke. I had
heard him color it with pity, and once or twice with awe,
but never before had he said it with so much terror.

He shivered, though the day was growing warmer.

"Women!" he said. "This place is full of women."

His eyes had the bluish cast of age, but his teeth were

strong and white, and he still had hair enough to comb. Fuzz was sprouting from his ears. I wondered if mother cut it for him sometimes? Age brings a set of new intimacies to a relationship. We don't love old men the same way we love young ones. When all our hungry desire, all our pride and burning hope and anger is gone, when old men outlive the heroes, the love that remains is almost too tender to bear. Standing there, eye to eye with my father's fear, I could have wept for him.

"You see how it is?" he said. "Only the men die."

14

CONCLUSION: MANTALK

There are societies where men speak a language among themselves, women speak another, and when the sexes address each other it is in a third mode. There are also languages where the form of a verb changes according to the sex under discussion or the one speaking; and all languages commonly spoken have pronouns that designate gender. In English, many adjectives descriptive of a sister are not normally applied to her brother: "leggy," "bubbly," and "ballbreaking," for example. Come to that, will anyone ever call her "craggy," "lionhearted," or a "prick"?

It's not hard to understand why some feminists hope that by changing language they can change history to "herstory" or even "itstory." Nevertheless, no number of "chair-people" or "househusbands" are going to alter a tool that has grown to accommodate us as we have been, as we pretty much continue to be, and as we are becoming. Language is our own invention and in order to change it at all we must first change ourselves. Language is more than words. It is also inflection and innuendo. I have frequently heard myself called "Ms" in a tone of such scorn I would have preferred "Miss" or even "hey, you." A heterosexual man speaking to another man in Western Mantalk does not use the same voice or posture he does when speaking to a woman. Furthermore, a man speaking to an alluring woman does not present himself as he does to a woman who is older, smarter, or taller.

Males are honest and instinctive in their response to the opposite sex. They size up every woman as a potential sexual playmate, which in truth has always been one of the female's primary roles. It is women these days who aren't sure how they want men to address them while at the same time depending as much as ever for their own definition upon the masculine response to them. Does a modern woman want to be a desirable object, addressed by a man with his head inclined and his nose bathed in her perfume? Does she want to be seen as an equal, from a cool distance, spoken to in jargon and casual obscenities? Does she hold herself to be a man's superior, so while he speaks to her his eye wanders, he shifts in place, and shows himself eager to be gone? Men are attuned to the feminine message because it tells them whether a sexual pass will be rejected or not; however, at the moment, the message being sent out by women is confusing, and men are showing the strain.

Mantalk is becoming a defensive, secret language, subversive to the female's worldly ambitions. Men in positions of power are trying to obfuscate the rules of the game and hide under a garment of words and clues primary issues women are accustomed to treat with common sense. When an American spokesman says of a Central American nation, for instance: "To hold free elections would require them to cross an ideological threshold they are not yet willing to cross," it is Mantalk that defies any but the initiated to understand he means "they're bad guys and we're good guys who believe all men have equal rights except them. . . ." Or when a senator says of the President: "It would be less than honest, and unrealistic, for him to lock himself into a no-tax-under-any-condition position," it requires a woman to triumph over her fear of feeling unlovable and over her need to respect the speaker for her to hear him mean that we're in money trouble and our elected leader is a liar. Though women have always nursed the dying and laid out the dead, they are unlikely to think their service and intuition is needed in what a health report to a government committee last year called, in Mantalk, "the overall mortality experience."

Language develops according to the circumstances in which it is spoken, and Mantalk is rarely heard at home. Men stand unnoticed on the thresholds of rooms where women are talking, and after listening for a few perplexed moments, they turn away like ineffectual ghosts. When men gather to talk, it is more likely to be at a clubroom or a boardroom or a bar than in a room of the house. There is something a little suspect when men gather inside the home like spies or anarchists or conspirators. Moreover, there is no room in most modern houses suited to prolonged Mantalk. Men cannot gather in the kitchen where interruptions are constant and distracting. Living rooms and parlors are common rooms with a propriety about them that discourages blunt outbursts of Mantalk; and to collect in bedrooms where the furnishings are suggestive of eroticism is unthinkable. As for bathrooms, when they are private, not only are they small and uncomfortable but to be seen emerging from them together or en masse would be scandalous. When bathrooms and toilets are public, men can have hurried, innocent conversations, though lacking the excuse of mirrors and mascara, they cannot linger the way women do. Unless a man is rich enough to have a billiard room, or a den, or a study, he won't be able to exchange much Mantalk in his own home. Even if his income runs to a room of his own, the comings and goings of his fellows will be screened, as a man is hardly ever alone in the family home.

Men do not speak softly to each other. Because Mantalk

is largely concerned with displaying evidence of the speaker's status, it must be spoken at a volume that approaches broadcasting. Once the speaker has captured the attention of other men he can throw himself wholeheartedly into the performance until he is pushed out of center stage by the next man. It is at this point, when a woman tries to enter the conversation, which means in Mantalk to dominate it for a while, she is called shrill and is dismissed for her tone, if not her words. Mantalk is the antithesis of whispering. Its vocabulary is tailored to anecdote and the re-creation of triumphs, while women dissect private behavior and analyze personal emotions. In spite of sometimes being mutually incomprehensible these are not incompatible languages. The things men say and the things women say, together say it all.

Men and women are different creatures. Everything reflects that difference, and everything depends on it. There is a part of each sex's experience that is closed to the other through no fault on either side. Nature isn't fair, but that need not stop us from trying to be fair to each other, which means we must try to hear each other out and not deny the other's perception of life. It is difference, not likeness or equality, that produces progress, and it is friction that produces excitement. When the sexes do find love, its source will turn out to be sublime acceptance of each other's differences.